Chalk Dust

Chalk Dust

A TEACHER'S MARKS

DAVID ELLISON

HEINEMANN
PORTSMOUTH, NH

Heinemann
A division of Reed Elsevier Inc.
361 Hanover Street
Portsmouth, NH 03801–3912
www.heinemann.com

Offices and agents throughout the world

All essays were previously published between 1991 and 1999 in *The Angus* (Almeda Newspaper Group), Fremont, California.

Library of Congress Cataloging-in-Publication Data
Ellison, David, 1959–
    Chalk dust : a teacher's marks / David Ellison.
        p. cm.
    Consists of essays previously published between 1991 and 1999 in *The Angus*, Fremont, California.
    ISBN 0-325-00558-3 (pbk. : alk. paper)
    1. Teaching—United States. I. Angus (Fremont, Calif.). II. Title.
    LB1775.2 .E44 2003
    371.1—dc21   2002151788

Editor: Lois Bridges
Production: Lynne Reed
Cover design: Jenny Jensen Greenleaf
Typesetter: Tom Allen
Manufacturing: Jamie Carter

Printed in the United States of America on acid-free paper
07   06   05   04   03   VP   1   2   3   4   5

For Michael,
my student,
whom Life cheated,
then abandoned.

For all the Michaels . . .

Contents

Contents

Contents

Prologue

CHALK DUST: A TEACHER'S MARKS WAS BORN AMID MANY A heated discussion with my brothers. Despite the fact that they had never so much as stepped foot in a public school, they knew precisely how to manage and improve one. "Fail 'em!" they'd blithely prescribe for my struggling students.

However, once I told an anecdote about my daily experience in the classroom, and in particular about my relationship with kids, once I put names and faces to the issue, my brothers responded with a far more humble, "Oh, I had no idea." Then, after a thoughtful silence, "You know, Dave, you ought to write these stories down."

And the rest, as they say, is history. Eventually I wrote nearly three hundred stories and opinion pieces for a local newspaper, *The Argus*, part of the San Francisco Bay Area's Alameda Newspaper Group; seventy-two appear in the succeeding pages.

Chalk Dust loosely chronicles my twenty-year career as an educator. After a stint teaching English part time in northern Spain, I chose to postpone for a few more foolish years a real career. And so, in 1983, despite my father's silent disapproval, I undertook a sixth-grade class at St. Leo's Grade School on the south side of San Antonio, Texas. I taught everything from math to religion and, as I had no formal training, learned from my mistakes, which were many. Two years later I moved to tiny St. Gerard's High on the east side, where I taught Spanish and English. Eventually, my dad and I realized my irresponsible play was, in fact, my life's calling. I came to California for a master's and a teaching credential. Then, in 1988, I arrived at

Barnard-White Middle School in Union City, California, where I've worked since as a teacher, mentor, and administrator.

I'm still learning from my mistakes, and still musing about them in writing. Often, only as I write, do I finally realize how powerfully an unfortunate student or difficult situation has affected me.

My joy as an educator endures, though, which I myself recognize anew during occasional moments of blessed self-awareness. A week ago, for example, just after the bell for first period had rung, I stepped outside to unlatch and close the classroom door. I glanced briefly at the sun gilding the eastern hills, savored a deep breath, and thanked God that I got to walk back through that door and spend my day with kids.

So, turn the page, and follow me through that door . . .

Acknowledgments

I MUST THANK JACK LYNESS, THE *ARGUS* EDITOR, WHO FIRST TOOK a chance on the "mousy" character who showed up a day late for his interview. I am similarly grateful to Lois Bridges and the other Heinemann editors who, although recognizing *Chalk Dust* was a "big risk," threw caution to the wind and published it.

Then, of course, there are all those who have patiently listened to my stories over the years, especially my mom and my family who spent their summer vacation helping choose which articles to include; Uncle Fred and Aunt Marge whom I'll forever emulate; Paul, who not only encouraged my story-telling but came up with the book's subtitle; and Kevin who assiduously edited so many terribly frivolous modifiers.

Finally, there are all the students, teachers, and administrators with whom I've lived and worked these past twenty years. They've tolerated me, taught me, and filled my days with laughter, challenges, and meaning. *Chalk Dust* is their story.

Chalk
Dust

Desiderata

WHEN I FIRST STARTED TEACHING, I MADE A POINT OF DRESSING casually. Young, idealistic, I rebelled against the pervasive image-conscious culture that judged a person by such a frivolous criteria as clothes. I typically sported faded corduroys, a striped polo shirt with a frayed collar, and a pair of dilapidated Keds. I would earn respect with my competence, my skills and ability.

Nonetheless, when parents dropped their children off and spied the slovenly character to whom they were entrusting their children, they weren't exactly assured. "He did go to college, didn't he?" one murmured apprehensively. And all the hapless principal could offer in defense was, "He seemed OK during the phone interview."

You see, I wasn't an easy new teacher for any principal to direct.

When Halloween came, for example, and everyone wore an outlandish outfit to school, I showed up in my best suit and tie. "I'm masquerading as a teacher," I explained with a smirk. The principal shook his head and shuffled away muttering to himself. That was his usual response to my antics.

A few weeks later I interrupted my students' lunchtime keep-away game. "All right! All right! Give me the ball," I scolded in feigned anger, as if I'd caught the kids tackling again. Once I had the ball in hand, though, my frown gave way to a mischievous grin. "I'm it," I laughed, and took off running.

Well, I was fast. I kept that class at bay for nearly five minutes before cunning little Conrad blindsided me, and brought me panting to the ground.

Then the kids showed no mercy. At the end of lunch, I limped disheveled past the principal, one Keds missing, dried grass hanging from my hair and stuffed down my shirt, my students prancing triumphantly around me. He shook his head and shuffled away, muttering to himself.

In the spring, it was my class' turn to perform at the PTA meeting, and so lure parents into attending. There would be no boring songs or puppet shows for us! No, I convinced my students we needed to do something really unique.

Little Jennifer took the stage. Reverently opening a ponderous text, she began to read "The Desiderata": "Go placidly amid the noise and the haste . . ."

Then, little by little, according to my meticulous directions, all hell broke loose on stage. A baby dropped his lollipop and wailed. His mother shrieked at him to stop. Bank robbers entered, shooting their cap guns, pursued by policemen blowing their whistles. Dogs barked. Elvis sang.

And all the while Jennifer read, oblivious: "And whether or not it is clear to you, no doubt the universe is unfolding as it should. . . ."

Meanwhile, Conrad slowly assembled a huge bomb in the center of the stage.

In the end, there was a gigantic crash, the lights went out, silence prevailed.

A few moments later the lights came back on revealing Jennifer serenely finishing her reading, "It is still a beautiful world . . ." while the rest of my students lay helter-skelter on stage in various grotesque poses of death.

I thought it was brilliant. The parents in attendance, though, after a stunned moment of disbelief, merely applauded perfunctorily.

Hurt, I asked the principal what he thought of the performance.

"Dave," he sighed in exasperation, "it was very . . . you."
Then he shook his head and shuffled away, muttering to himself.

That was a compliment, right?

Coup de Grace

"MR. ELLISON, YOU DON'T KNOW NOTHING ABOUT WHAT GOES on in this class," Liz announced defiantly.

Even today, twenty years later, her words haunt me. How many times have I imagined I'd responded with something clever or witty, put her in her place, asserted my authority? But all I could muster then was, "Sit down, Liz, and get back on-task."

She smirked, hesitated just long enough to demonstrate her contempt for me, and then sat smugly down, another victory won.

Liz humiliated me quite often that year. She was quite adept at it. In fact, she and her sixth-grade minions had driven off two teachers the previous year, forcing them to resign mid-semester. She must have salivated when I, so naively enthusiastic, walked blithely in. It was my first teaching job. She immediately set out to make it my last.

And there I was, a month later, struggling in vain to contain Liz and her wicked designs. I had to admit—bitterly—that she was right: I really didn't know what was going on.

Oh, but Liz did! For instance, she organized an elaborate parent-signature forging ring, ensuring that bad news never made it home. Similarly, she often arranged for certain students' names to disappear off the blackboard detention list whenever I turned my back. For a while, she even scheduled regular water fights in the girls' restroom. It sure did seem like she was in charge.

No matter what I tried in order to regain control or establish a more positive atmosphere in class, Liz found a way to undermine it. The Missing Tapes Incident stands out. I'd invited the kids to bring in cassette tapes of their favorite music, which I played softly each day while they wrote in their journals. I'd hoped this would induce everyone to enjoy the activity, and perhaps even to believe I was a "cool" teacher after all. For a few days, it looked like I was succeeding.

But Liz couldn't allow that. One day the tapes mysteriously disappeared off my desk.

I was furious! This time, I vowed, I wouldn't let Liz win. I initiated an exhaustive dragnet, conducted myriad interrogations, and slowly but surely began to unravel her network. When she realized she would soon be implicated, though, she coerced Sammy, one of the shyest kids in class, to take the rap. Dutifully, he did. He was more afraid of Liz than a two-day suspension.

Liz was only twelve, but I hated her! I was so young, though, so inexperienced. I made so many mistakes. Nonetheless, I kept on trying; and I guess that's why, even though I never won her obedience, I finally did earn her grudging respect.

It was the last day of school. The books were collected, the walls bare, and all that remained was for me to say good-bye to the class. Once again, I could think of nothing to say. I was exhausted, and terribly disappointed with the year. I thought I was a failure.

That's when Liz stood up again. I braced myself for her coup de grace.

"I'll say one thing for you, Mr. Ellison," she said evenly. "You never gave up."

Those, Liz's final words to me, made that whole terrible year worthwhile.

A Smile

ROBERT WASN'T THE SHORTEST SIXTH GRADER I TAUGHT, BUT HE was the pudgiest, the slowest. As a result, just as I had been in middle school, he was picked last for every team. He tried to compensate by excelling elsewhere, in math.

It was inspiring, yet worrisome to see him struggling so hard. Not really all that gifted, Robert nonetheless refused to accept any score less than an A. He constantly asked questions, often stayed after school for extra help, and typically studied for hours every evening. (In that respect, he and I were nothing alike!) Still, a B+ was all he could manage.

Worst of all, Robert took no joy in any of his efforts. He became frustrated, almost panicky if he didn't understand a concept right away. A difficult problem was not a fascinating challenge, but a frightening assault on his precarious sense of self-worth. It was as if a single intellectual stumble might destroy him. He never smiled.

"Relax, Robert," I told him. "Take a stress pill! Laugh a little. An A in math isn't everything, you know."

But for Robert it was.

Then, one day I announced I'd be coaching the track team and urged everyone to sign up. (My first coaching job!) Robert rushed up to me after class, furious. "Who's going to tutor me after school? How could you do this to me?"

I suspected he was concerned about a lot more than just his math score. In his eyes I had betrayed him, gone over to the other side—athletics—where he could not follow.

"No problem, Robert," I replied. "Just join the team. We'll study after practice."

He was silent a few moments, and then mumbled dejectedly, "Come on, Mr. Ellison. You know I can't run."

"Nonsense! I'll see you after school and show you."

To everyone's amazement and my delight, Robert showed up.

I led the team leisurely around a short course through the neighborhood. Once the school was again in sight, though, I fell back and found Robert walking, gasping. I put my arm around him and, ignoring his vigorous objections, forced him to jog the last hundred meters.

"It hurts so much, Mr. Ellison!" he sobbed.

"I know, Robert. But three weeks from now it won't. And next year you won't finish last either."

Well, to make a long story short, Robert came to every practice that spring, each afternoon running a little bit easier, a tad bit faster. In fact, Robert continued to push himself all through the summer, and showed up the next fall forty pounds lighter. I could barely recognize him.

There was no wonderful, melodramatic ending, though. Robert didn't go on to win the final race of the next season. Nor did he earn his long-coveted A in math. He remained ever-determined, but ever dissatisfied.

I still think about Robert a lot. I have no doubt that, wherever he is, he's working hard. I trust he's still running. I hope that, if he hasn't managed to be the best at something, at least he's satisfied with his best. Above all, I pray he's learned to smile. And I like to imagine I had something to do with it.

A Whimper

JAMES REMINDED ME OF SOME BEDRAGGLED DOG THAT, NO matter how much mistreatment he endures, adores his cruel master all the more for it. You see, James loved his father deeply, but feared him even more. He did everything in his power to satisfy him, yet it was never enough.

James' dad was a recruiting sergeant for the Marines. He expected—no demanded—that James and his older brother have the "mettle" to be among the few and the proud. Indeed, he treated them with the same high expectations, the same strict, cold discipline he did his recruits. I never once saw him laugh, nor even relax. Come to think of it, I never saw James do so either.

James' older brother seemed none the worse for his upbringing. An honor-roll student and star quarterback, he was talented, handsome, and cocky. He brought home many trophies, which he laid solemnly at the feet of his father. He was the perfect son, in whom his dad was well pleased. (I didn't like him.)

Oh, how James struggled to be the same! Despite the fact that he was slow in mind and body, he was heroically persistent. He tried out for every team. He labored with each school assignment. He never made the cut, though. He never made the grade. Worst of all, he never made his father proud.

One day James stopped by my desk after class. "Please, Mr. Ellison, let me take the history quiz over. I can't get a D. I just can't! I'll study even harder this time, I promise!"

I understood his desperation. Parent–teacher conferences loomed the following week. We studied together that afternoon, painstakingly recopying and reviewing his notes. James strained to grasp, to remember.

He took the make-up quiz after school the following day, while I corrected papers at my desk. After a few minutes, I looked up to give him a smile of encouragement, only to spy him furtively conceal a scrap of paper beneath the quiz. No, I thought. Please, no.

I went over to his desk, and asked him to move his quiz aside. Sure enough, there was his cheat sheet. "James," I whispered, shaking my head with dread.

The next moment seemed too dramatic, too full of tragic pathos for real life. It belonged in some sort of movie like *Stand and Deliver*, not in my mundane classroom.

Tears flooded James' eyes, dropping in large, ponderous drops onto his quiz. All he could manage, between sobs which shook his body, was, "I try so hard to please my father. I try . . . so hard. . . ."

"I know, James," I said, incapable of consoling him. "I know." I had never before seen anyone despair so utterly.

When I met with James and his dad the next week, I didn't mention the cheating. Instead, I described how hard James had been working, how very proud I was of him.

"Well, Mr. Ellison," James' dad said severely, "apparently my standards are much higher than yours." Then he stood abruptly and left. James slunk meekly behind, with his tail between his legs—and, I imagined, a whimper.

Miss Donelson

I LIED TO MISS DONELSON. I LIED ABOUT HER. I EVEN CONVINCED myself for a time that I hated her. I was such a jerk!

I'm sure Miss Donelson was pleasant enough that first day of my Freshman History class. But, as far as I was concerned, she'd committed a mortal sin, for which there could be no forgiveness. She'd insisted, despite what I perceived to be an absolutely stifling heat, that I button my collar and straighten my tie—as was befitting a proper young man in a Jesuit high school.

Why I made such a fuss I still cannot fathom. But I told all my friends that Miss Donelson was a mean, nasty, totally unreasonable, and downright ruthless tyrant.

Of course, the matter of the tie was not enough to substantiate such a scathing review. So, whenever necessary, I simply invented new and terrible stories about her. I invented so much and so often that pretty soon I could no longer distinguish my facts from my fabrications—not that such distinctions mattered as long as I tarnished her reputation.

It was inevitable that Miss Donelson would one day hear of my stories. On another sweltering day she asked to see me after class. One by one, she recounted every last lie. I stood there, fidgeting, avoiding her eyes, finally speechless. She gave me no lecture or punishment. She simply made me remain there for a few moments of unbearable embarrassment. And then, with an amused smile, she allowed me to slink away.

I wish I could say I'd mended my ways after that. I was a lot more careful with my lies. But I despised Miss Donelson more than ever. Indeed, although I could not claim credit for her nickname, "Ann of a Thousand Thighs," I propagated it throughout the school.

The amazing thing was that, despite everything I did, Miss Donelson still liked me. Oh, she knew I was a jerk. But she had faith that I would eventually grow up.

Deep down, in spite of my professed hatred for her, I knew she liked me. I suppose that's why I tried to make her proud in the end. Why else would I have struggled for so long on my final project for her my junior year?

I finally did grow up, and now a lot of my students are jerks. (Sometimes there is justice in the world!) They lie to me and about me. They've even invented some terribly cruel—but very amusing—nicknames for me. ("Roll-On," a sinister reference to the top of my head, is my favorite.) Sometimes I'd like to yell and scream at them. But then I remember how immature I was, and how patient Miss Donelson remained. Because I remember, I can often overlook my students' silly, sometimes maddening behavior. I like my students anyway.

I have Miss Donelson to thank for that. And if the jerks I teach knew about her, they'd thank her too.

Bless Us Oh Lord . . .

I'D LIKE TO PROPOSE AN ALTERNATIVE TO THE NATIONAL DAY OF School Prayer.

Don't get me wrong. With sixteen years of Catholic education, and then five more teaching in Catholic schools, I've done more than my share of classroom praying. And, given the homogeneous enrollment at those schools and their obvious religious mission, the prayer was quite appropriate.

Nonetheless, despite the daily Hail Mary's, weekly liturgies, and monthly penances of my youth, I cannot recall one single instance of real communion with God at school. Nor did all that pious prattle seem to strengthen my character or that of my friends because, quite honestly, we were hellions.

On the other hand, there were three indelible experiences in my life that did instill a profound reverence for prayer; and they each involved a rare glimpse at another faith.

In high school, my history teacher showed the film *Fiddler on the Roof*—the bittersweet, tender story of a Jewish village in Russia. Saturday night, just at sundown, families gathered around the Sabbath candles. Chanting, singing, they rekindled their faith in God and each other. I compared their sacred ritual with my family's hasty mealtime "Bless us oh Lord, and these thy gifts . . . ," and I was ashamed.

Many years later, while wandering through Spain, I met a Buddhist. We traveled together to Santiago de Compastela, where I observed him approach on his knees the crypt where St. James' remains supposedly lay. "The faith of millions of pilgrims over the ages has made this ground sacred," he whispered in response to my quizzical glance. Then he sat impassive for more than an hour. "No, I don't recite anything," he explained afterwards. "I strive to create a silence within me, so that I may one day truly listen." His devout patience humbled me.

A year later I taught sixth grade in Texas. After I'd finished The Crusades, I was frustrated that my students continued to view the epoch—and all history, in fact—in simplistic good versus evil terms (Christians good, Muslims bad!), even though my lessons had included an unbiased review of Islam. So I invited a Muslim to class.

At one poignant moment, he carefully spread some construction paper on the floor, knelt down upon it facing east, and solemnly pressed his forehead to the floor. "Now, to whom am I praying?" he queried the kids.

"To Allah!" they responded with enthusiasm.

"No," the visitor replied intently, "to God—your God, my God. We call Him 'Allah,' you call Him 'Jesus'; but He is one, He is great, He made and loves us all."

That day my students finally understood how tragically misguided The Crusades were. Also, we all pledged we'd genuflect at church Sunday morning a little less perfunctorily.

I propose we provide every child a similar experience: A National Day of Religions, an opportunity once a year for students of all faiths and traditions, not to pray, but to share with each other how and why they do pray—or even why they don't.

I suspect that, not only would kids come to know and respect each other more; but, once they returned to their families, churches, synagogues, mosques . . . they'd all pray with renewed fervor.

(And, just maybe, there might be fewer hellions!)

High Standards

I LEARNED A REMARKABLE LESSON MANY YEARS AGO, ONE WHICH has served me well ever since, and which I hope will do the same for new teachers as they embark on their first year in the classroom.

I had just begun a new job teaching Spanish in a small, Catholic high school in San Antonio, Texas. Unfortunately, Spanish was only an elective there, and so was considered a fluffy, easy course.

My predecessor, for example, had been anything but strict. She had rarely assigned homework, but had almost always given her students at least a B, whether they could speak any Spanish or not, the latter being predominately the case. It seemed as if she had made an unspoken pact with her students: She wouldn't force them to really learn anything as long as they behaved. Everyone had appeared content.

Then I arrived. I announced the first day that I would give homework every night, and not one, but two quizzes a week; and that, after a brief introduction, I'd ban English in class.

Jaws hung open, eyes grew wide, and heads slowly shook. Several students immediately dropped my class. The rest fought me bitterly. In fact, the principal remarked dryly at the first staff meeting that I had earned a dubious distinction: After only one week, my name had already made it on the bathroom walls.

Then a strange thing happened: My students learned some Spanish. In fact, they began to jokingly call out phrases like

Cállate (Shut up!) and *Date prisa* (Hurry up!) in the lunchroom and hallways. Soon they were tossing around complete sentences; and for some of them, Spanish became a secret language they flaunted among their monolingual friends.

The clincher came in the spring when I organized a student-exchange program with a high school in Monterey, Mexico. Somehow—sometimes haltingly, often with grammar that made me wince—my students managed to communicate. I was so proud of them, and they were proud of themselves.

Don't get me wrong. The following year my students still came to my class groaning, and my name still graced the bathroom walls.

One dramatic, very important thing had changed though: There were twice as many kids in my classes. All of them realized I'd push them hard, give them regular homework and quizzes. Yet they also knew they would learn. And so they came, complaining the whole while, but they came.

That's the lesson I've never forgotten: Despite all their protests to the contrary, kids really do desire to learn. They want us to be hard on them.

So don't make the typical new-teacher mistake of seeking popularity by being easy. You'll fail. You see, students understand, at least intuitively, that holding them to high standards is the greatest compliment we can pay them; and that to do anything else is to insult them most insidiously.

Indeed, I suspect that my long-lost students from San Antonio now remember me much more than they do that first, easy teacher. What is much more important, I bet they remember some Spanish too.

The Peter Principal

"MAURICE PROVES THE PETER PRINCIPLE WRONG," I WROTE bitterly in my journal. "He has risen far above his level of incompetence."

Rotund, with thick spectacles, a bristly mustache, and a wardrobe straight from the racks of The Goodwill, Maurice shared a preparation period with me in the small Catholic high school in Texas where I taught Spanish eighteen years ago. One May morning he stormed into the staff room and blurted out, "God-damned seniors! They don't give a shit about anything! I can't teach them a fucking thing! I'm going to show them videos the rest of the year." And he did.

Maurice taught Theology.

Unfortunately, Maurice typified the rest of the faculty. The English teacher (basketball coach), for example, usually read the newspaper while his students worked on their "independent study" projects. The math teacher (head football coach) arrived late to class, read out a page from the textbook in a deadly drawl, randomly assigned some homework problems, and then retreated to his scouting videos. The principal (defensive football coach), flirted brazenly with the cheerleaders, and promptly dropped all the athletes from my class once I dared to fail one of them.

I was on the verge of quitting in disgust when, to my surprise and glee, the principal abruptly announced his resignation. "Geez," I muttered to myself, "with a dynamic principal this could be a good school." I decided the possibility was worth a gamble, signed a contract for another year, and waited with baited breath for the school board to hire a new principal.

They chose Maurice.

I ranted and raved in my journal, moped and despaired around the house, but finally resigned myself to another year of absurdity.

That fall, however, in the middle of an interminable staff meeting, Maurice did something remarkable. He announced that all grades must be turned in directly to him. He would compile the athlete-eligibility list himself, deleting the names of those students with two or more Fs. He actually intended to enforce the school's rules!

The coaches' temper tantrum was spectacular, yet Maurice braved it stolidly. Not long afterwards, he removed the newspaper from the English class, and returned the athletes to mine. By June, he'd transformed himself and the school. Who'd have thought?

Certainly not Maurice. At the graduation ceremony, he stood awkwardly at the podium, used his tie to clumsily polish his glasses, and then, in a faltering, painfully sincere voice, addressed the students: "I think I know how y'all feel. You're scared. I sure was when I took this job last year. I didn't think I could do it. I suppose I wasn't alone in that belief.

"Look. I'm still here. I'm still scared, but I'm very proud.

"Fear is good, you know. It means we're daring to risk, to push ourselves beyond what we think are our limits. And it's only by doing so that we can discover who we really are.

"Trust me. Despite your terrible doubts, you too are all capable of a greatness neither you nor anyone else can even imagine. And what an adventure it is to discover it!"

So, in the end, I was ironically prophetic. Maurice did indeed prove the Peter Principle wrong. May we all do likewise.

One Heck of a Romance

As with the biblical story of the ten lepers, very few of my students ever return to say "Thank you." Still, over the years, some have written, and I treasure their letters above all else. Whenever my commitment or confidence falters, I reread them to remind myself that I've made a difference with at least a few of my students.

Out of all the letters, Christine's is my favorite. Perhaps this is so because I never expected to receive one like it. When I used to teach high school Spanish, I'd hoped one of my students would one day write with the news she had passed the Advanced Placement Exam, or had gone on to become an ambassador to a Latin American country. Christine, however, related quite a different tale:

> . . . I also wanted to tell you about what happened to me last summer. Me, my mom, and my brother went to Martinique for a week. While we were there I had to use my Spanish.
>
> I was waiting for dinner to start, and I went for a walk on the beach. It was a beautiful night. Up behind me comes a nice-looking guy, and says, "Parlez vous Francais?"
>
> I said, "No, I'm an American. I speak English. Do you speak English?" He said no. Then he asked me if I spoke Spanish. I said a little.
>
> I hadn't spoken Spanish since school got out, but everything you taught me came rushing back into my head. We talked for hours in Spanish on the beach, and one thing led to another and, well, you know. . . . I mean, we didn't "YOU KNOW," but, well, we made-out for several hours! It was one heck of a romance.

Anyway, it would never have happened if I hadn't known Spanish as well as I did, which was all because of you.

Now I can die in peace.

Seriously, I love Christine's letter. Not only does it bring a smile to my face when I'm down; but I used to put it to good use in my Spanish classes. I had often sought to motivate my students by reminding them how important Spanish is—how, for example, the ability to speak it could open up so many career opportunities.

Well, this impassioned speech of mine was almost invariably greeted with yawns. Then I tried reading my students part of Christine's letter. It was the strangest thing: Suddenly they studied with renewed vigor and enthusiasm. . . .

No Regrets

"I GUESS I JUST HAD A GOOD DAY LAST FRIDAY," KIM RESPONDED with exaggerated innocence. Of course, we both knew she was lying through her teeth. With a dismal 40 percent average in Spanish, she had somehow managed a miraculous 95 percent on the previous Friday's quiz. Such an instantaneous improvement was impossible.

I figured she had probably arranged to have a friend in my morning class copy down the quiz questions on his cover sheet, and share them with her over lunch. I couldn't prove that; so I had her take the same quiz again. Surprise, surprise: She scored her customary 40 percent.

I had hoped that, when confronted with the discrepancy in scores, Kim could engage in an honest, mature discussion. She was a senior after all. Shamefaced, she would apologize for cheating. Indignant, I would give her a zero on the quiz. Then, working together, we'd plan a strategy to prepare her for the final exam.

But, no, she just smiled and insisted that Friday had been her lucky day. I thought I couldn't be more disappointed. She would prove me wrong.

During the next few weeks, Kim declined my frequent offers to tutor her. Instead, she chose to rely on her southern, Texas charm. She greeted me ever so sweetly each afternoon. During class she frequently offered to answer the easy questions; and then smiled broadly, as if to say, "See how hard I'm trying?" But when it came to doing homework, or trying to really learn to speak or understand Spanish—*nada*. (Which means, Kim, "nothing.")

That was never more evident than when Kim took the fateful, final exam. I wasn't surprised when she left most of it blank. I was impressed, though, with the lengthy letter she wrote me on the back.

She had tried so very hard, she claimed; but, gosh, she just couldn't seem to remember those funny words. Still, she had really enjoyed my class, and I was her favorite teacher. Did I know, she asked, she was also failing science? Another F in Spanish would prevent her from walking the stage at graduation. Surely, I didn't want that! There was so much more she wanted to say. "Perhaps," she offered, "we could meet together after school. I know I can find a way to convince you."

I'm sure she could. But I never gave her the chance. I gave her, instead, the F she so richly deserved.

Kim still had one more trick up her sleeve. Before I turned in my grades to the office, she joined the Graduation Planning Committee. She signed up for everything, including the second reading. It was a clever plan. By the time the principal received the list of Fs, her name would already have been printed in the graduation program. Then we'd have to let her participate. Or, so she'd hoped.

Well, Kim was partially successful. Her name did appear in the program. But she did not appear on stage.

It was a shame, given how very bright and resourceful Kim was. (If only she had directed some of that creative energy toward her studies!)

You know, I've had to fail many students over the years. But Kim was the only student I ever failed without regret.

Smart

DEAR STUDENTS,

When I first decided to become a teacher, I thought I would meet a few smart students, a few dumb ones, and a lot in between. Some kids were destined by their genes (or genius) to excel in school. Others would fail no matter what I or they themselves tried to do. Fate was terribly cruel. Or, so I believed.

Many of you, I know, share that faith in academic predestination. "He's getting an A because he's smart," you say. "I could never do so well, even if I tried." You shrug your shoulders and reconcile yourselves to your Cs and Ds. It's a bitter pill to swallow, but comforting in a way. It leaves a sweet aftertaste of complacency.

Well, my students, I've got some discomforting news. I think we've been deceiving ourselves. During the last twenty years, I've taught thousands of kids of all ages. I have yet to meet one who couldn't succeed if he or she really tried. Oh, I've failed more than a few of them. But they weren't dumb. They were lazy, or had allowed themselves to become intellectually weak. Fate had nothing to do with it.

Intellectual ability isn't, like the color of your eyes, determined at birth. Your mind is like a muscle. If you use it a lot, it will become stronger and stronger. But, if you cease to challenge your mind—if, for example, you watch the typical three hours of television a day—soon your mind will become flabby and weak. You'll be unable to accomplish even the most simple of intellectual tasks. You aren't smart or dumb, you see. You work hard, or you do not.

There are students blessed with special abilities, of course. Some are naturally adept at jumping hurdles, while others can effortlessly solve quadratic equations. Nonetheless, all kids can compete both on the track and in the classroom if they try. In fact, I've seen "slow" kids beat an apparently faster or smarter peer time and time again. They just worked a lot harder.

I asked an Olympic trainer once which was more important in order to become an outstanding athlete, natural talent or hard work. "A champion," he responded, "owes 90 percent of her success to simple blood, sweat, and tears."

I'm sorry, kids. The same is true for you.

Why do I find myself apologizing for what ought to be good news? You should be overjoyed to hear that fate has not set a limit to your potential. With consistent effort, you can accomplish almost anything you set your mind to do!

Ah, but there's the rub. If your success or failure in school is not fated, then you haven't an excuse. You must choose. You must decide whether to accept the responsibility and, above all, the work—years of hard work. It's no wonder that many of you might want to shy away from the challenge, or pretend it just isn't there.

Stop looking for excuses and, as the Nike commercial urges, "Just do it!" Turn off the tube. Pick up a book. Ask questions. Study every night, and take pride in your assignments. It will be difficult at first. Before you know it, though, your mind will be strong, and your success will be easy. People will say it's because you're smart. You and I will know the truth.

A Scarlet Letter

SANDY WAS A QUIET, STUDIOUS SENIOR IN MY SPANISH CLASS. Midway through the second semester, however, she mysteriously began to fail. She ignored my homework, and in class appeared strangely distracted. Even her shy smile had fled, leaving her morose, unhappy.

"What's the matter, Sandy?" I asked several times. Silence. "You know, don't you, that an F will prevent you from graduating? There's still plenty of time to catch up. Come on, Sandy! Don't drop the ball so close to the finish!"

She just sighed heavily, shrugged, and looked away.

I asked around, but, although her other teachers were similarly concerned, they were equally befuddled. Against their better judgment, I called Sandy's father. He merely heaped obscenities on both Sandy and me.

Then one day in May, Sandy disappeared. "She's in the hospital," answered one of the nuns in a furtive whisper. Yet, neither the good sister nor anyone else would elaborate. The secrecy made me both worried and intrigued.

Unfortunately, the truth—which Sandy later revealed to me herself—was worse than all my awful imaginings. Several months earlier she'd found herself pregnant. Overawed by the moralistic atmosphere of our Catholic school, where it was forbidden to discuss contraception, she'd been too afraid to confide in anyone. Even when she'd become seriously ill, she'd sought no help, preferring to guard her terrible sin in desperate, helpless silence.

One morning, Sandy finally collapsed and was rushed to the hospital, unconscious. The interns immediately recognized she was pregnant. They also discovered that her baby was dead. Inexplicably, its corpse had not been spontaneously aborted, but had remained in her womb, atrophying. The resulting blood poisoning had nearly killed her. Less than an hour after she entered the hospital, doctors performed an emergency hysterectomy. Sandy was seventeen years old.

When she awoke, she wished she were dead. Her father, repeatedly calling her a "whore," expressed the same desire.

Nonetheless, Sandy telephoned me only a few days later. "Mr. Ellison, I want to graduate. Will you tutor me?"

Sandy took slow, arduous steps down a sterile corridor to the hospital sunroom where we worked. She fought through the pain and the drugs to concentrate on conjugations, to complete my assignments. Later, when she received her diploma, her timid smile again adorned her face, and the entire school community rose to greet it with a standing ovation.

Although it seemed all had forsaken her, Sandy had persevered. And so, she'd transformed shame into self-respect, tragedy into triumph, a "Scarlet Letter" into a "Red Badge of Courage." Now, whenever I attend a graduation I remember Sandy, and the lessons she taught us all.

A Horrid Summer

It's painful to admit I was as much at fault as the kids. But time has given me a new perspective on that long, miserable nightmare we shared on Antigua in the West Indies. While it remains the worst summer of my life, I am wiser for the experience. At least, I know I'd be a better group leader if I were to do it again. Perhaps that is some consolation.

I had imagined the eleven high school students who accompanied me on the volunteer project would be naive, idealistic, intent on saving the world. My job would be to ease their disappointment when they realized they could barely make a difference in the small, local community. It was I, however, who would be disappointed.

I suspected something was wrong when I met the group. Hailing from the most affluent New England boarding schools, they tried to outdo each other with tales of their parents' wealth. Anne was the worst: "Why just the other day, when I was heading for lunch at Daddy's club as usual, my Beemer had a flat. Oh, it was an absolutely horrid day!"

I wanted to vomit. But things only got worse.

Two days later, I brought Anne to her morning volunteer project. She'd be working with children at the hospital. "But, Dave," she whispered, her lip quivering, "they're sick!"

"That's the idea, Anne," I responded impatiently. "These kids came here for long-term treatment. Many are far from home, and they're all lonely, scared, and bored. Just play with them or read to them. Help them forget their sickness.

They'll soon fall in love with you, Anne, and you with them. Trust me."

A few minutes later, though, when Anne spied one young boy who had been severely burned, her eyes rolled up in her head, and she fainted dramatically. The actor in me was impressed with the performance, but the project leader was growing exasperated.

Most of the other "volunteers" were no better. That evening, for instance, Gerald announced haughtily he wouldn't even consider eating the "vile" dinner one of the others had created. When it was Kimberly's turn to clean the bathroom, she refused, explaining, "I don't do bathrooms." Jonathan merely complained: "Why didn't they tell me the island was full of blacks?" Frankly, the only thing they were really interested in was either going to the beach, or necking out back.

Unfortunately, I did little to disguise my disgust. The group responded in kind, becoming even more obnoxious. When we finally left, I'm sure the whole island breathed a sigh of relief.

My final journal entry said it all: "I have infinite patience for disadvantaged kids. But I have none for these spoiled, selfish snobs. Good riddance!"

Today I read that with chagrin. For now I realize that wealthy students can be just as needy as poor ones, albeit in different, sometimes ugly ways. They, too, require patience and understanding. If only I had known that in Antigua, I might have enabled those kids to learn so much about the world and about themselves. But I didn't. And that's why I failed.

I only hope that, although Anne, for instance, surely has no fond memories of me, she does cherish a few of that small, burned boy, to whom she finally did read some stories.

Bitter Whispers

I'VE TRIED TO FORGET ABOUT STEVEN, HOW I LET HIM DOWN, leaving him utterly alone. But the gift he gave me, a clay statue of an Aztec king, still haunts me, denouncing me from atop my bookshelf even as I write this.

At the time, the statue seemed an appropriate Christmas gift for a high school Spanish teacher. But I now realize that nothing then was as it first appeared.

For example, nearly everyone considered Steven the most fortunate, enviable kid on campus. He was, after all, captain of the varsity track team. He excelled in all his classes too, especially mine.

Nonetheless, behind his easy success and his captivating smile, Steven hid a dark secret: He was gay.

He never told me, of course, at least not with words. Yet, in many other not-so-subtle ways, he revealed his desperate longing for acceptance, for companionship.

I recall the day Steven first sought me out. It was after I had admonished a classmate for jokingly insulting another with the epithet, "Faggot!"

"Pardon me," I chastised, "but that is very offensive, even in fun. It's just as bad as any racial slur—expressing prejudice against people who are different. I won't tolerate it in my class."

At the end of the period, Steven lingered to tell me I was the first teacher he'd met who'd ever defended homosexuals. After that, he stopped by often during lunch to chat, his questions becoming ever-more personal. Was I married? Was I presently dating anyone? He seemed pleased when, distracted, munching on my sandwich, I shook my head.

At Christmas, he timidly presented me with the statue. "I really like your class . . . and you, Mr. Ellison." Then he grasped me in a clumsy hug.

I was flattered. But I still didn't get it. Perhaps I didn't want to.

One evening a few weeks later, Steven came running up to me at a home basketball game. He insisted eagerly that I sit by him in the bleachers. But when I introduced him to a pretty woman at my side, his face collapsed. He stared at me wide-eyed, shaking his head in disbelief and betrayal. Then, after muttering a choked "Pleased to meet you, Miss," he fled the gym. At that awkward moment, I finally understood.

I wish I had followed him, or reached out at some other time. I should have broached the taboo subject, assured Steven he was not evil or weird, and above all, that he was not alone. But I was afraid. What teacher wouldn't be in a small, Catholic, homophobic high school in Texas?

I tried to laugh off the incident, to convince myself that I had misinterpreted Steven's behavior. He made it easy for me. He retreated obediently back into his murky closet, and never approached me again. Indeed, he even went on to become prom king! Surely he was not gay.

But Steven's gift, the Aztec king on my shelf, still whispers otherwise. And he reminds me bitterly that, in the end, I didn't deserve him.

Poe

WHEN I WAS A FRESHMAN IN COLLEGE AND SPIED THE SPECTER coming down the hall, he frightened me. Absurdly tall, with a large shock of unkempt black hair and a deeply lined, forbidding face, he swung his cane relentlessly to-and-fro in front of him. He seemed a bizarre morphing of an Edgar Allen Poe horror story, and an elongated, dreary El Greco painting. However, his gaping, vacuous eyes, which were forever tearing, as if from some terribly somber vision they alone could behold—yes, his eyes were the most unnerving. "Poe" was an apt name for him. Pity the poor undergrad who had him for a professor!

The first day second semester, I gasped silently when Poe entered my humanities seminar and, wiping his sightless eyes, introduced himself as Stephen Rogers, the instructor.

By spring break, however, I had a new name for him: "Tiresias," the blind seer, the implacable prophet. It had become obvious that it was I, not he, who was blind.

Patiently, sagely, Tiresias opened my eyes to The Great Books—works by Thucydides, Homer, Dante, Descartes, Kant, Shakespeare, Aquinas, Nietzsche —the "dead white men" now in such disrepute. I still recall as if it were yesterday his haunting reading of T.S. Eliot's poem "The Waste Land"—"April is the cruelest month, breeding lilacs out of the dead land, mixing memory and desire, stirring dull roots with spring rain. . . ."

For the first time, I began to appreciate the tremendous beauty of words and the power of the ideas they conveyed, even though I could still only barely understand them.

The next fall I changed my major to the liberal arts. "The arts of symbol-making and symbol-using," Tiresias explained, "the symbols we use to describe and ultimately to create our world, and ourselves."

"Pre-unemployment," my father lamented dryly. But Tiresias won out. You see, he awed me. Indeed, I was afraid to speak during my first few courses with him. Who wouldn't be in the presence of a prodigy who could nonchalantly recite obscure epic poems in five languages?

But, through a persistent mix of cajoling, goading, and easy laughter, Tiresias drew me out, igniting all the passion and curiosity I hadn't even known I possessed. Eventually he couldn't shut me up, and often accused me of throwing "intellectual hand grenades" in the midst of many class discussions.

Finally, one class I insisted on reading a passage from Plato's "Apology" aloud, Socrates' stoic response to the judges who'd sentenced him to die: "Death has caught me, the old man. Evil has caught you, the young. Now, I must suffer my fate, and you must suffer yours. . . ."

"That was very fine, David," Tiresias commented after a pause.

"Thanks, Doc," I responded flippantly. And this third nickname stuck. Doctor Stephen Rogers, alias "Doc," coached me through my final, tortuous forty-page senior essay on *The Psalms*. He engendered within my soul a fierce love of learning, a deep belief in the potential nobility of Man. And he gently nudged me in the direction of "the most honorable of all professions," teaching.

Poe, Tiresias, Doc . . .—he was my nightmare, my idol, and in the end my friend. He didn't just teach. He inspired. And that is what education is all about.

Beggars

It's humbling. I would like to say, when I signed on at Barnard-White Middle School as a history/Spanish teacher, I'd emerged from a large pool of qualified candidates, that I was simply the best of them all. The fact of the matter is, however, as my principal confided in me later, there was no one else.

I wish I had been more than my school's last and only resort.

Part of the problem is because many, many parents refuse to register their children on time, so public schools can only guess how many kids are going to show up in September. To save money, we usually guess low. From a financial point of view, it's much better to hire too few teachers than too many.

From an educational perspective, though, it's chaos. Every fall most public schools experience a mad, frenzied scramble, as we shuffle kids around, open new classes, and hunt for teachers to staff them. Beggars, of course, can't be choosers. Often we're lucky to find anyone to fill the new positions. (I'd been such an anyone.)

It's worse with math and science teachers. One year, for instance, one of the science teachers left in October. What a nightmare!

First we hired a long-term substitute to give us time to find a good, permanent replacement. One month later we were still empty-handed. In the end, we hired two student teachers as interns who split the position.

It was hardly the ideal situation. The student teachers, of

course, were thrilled at the opportunity to make some money and thus help pay for their extra year in college. But it would have been much better for them if they could have spent the year observing and team-teaching with master teachers. And, of course, no matter how successful the interns were, their students would have preferred veteran teachers.

We had no choice, though. We did our best to help the interns succeed, and then hoped for the best—knowing it wasn't our best.

Imagine, if we at Barnard-White have to struggle like this to find good teachers, despite the fine reputation our district enjoys—what must it be like in inner cities like Oakland and Los Angeles? What is worse, not only is there a scarcity of teachers, but the majority of those currently in the classroom scored near the bottom on every measure such as the SAT and GRE. There is some truth to that insidious adage, "Those who can't, teach. . . ." It's depressing, embarrassing, frightening.

That's why I often become impatient with debates about education reform. Most of the rhetoric ignores the most important issue: Who is teaching our kids? Good teachers will always find a way to help students learn, no matter what legislators might decree. But all the laws and testing in the world cannot transform not-so-good teachers into great ones. There simply is no substitute for great teachers. Unfortunately, there's no abundance of them either.

Joni's Tears

"OH DEAR GOD, WHAT HAVE I DONE?" JONI STOOD AT THE DOOR of her classroom, her first day at my school. The desks were empty, the bulletin boards bare, the room silent. And she was afraid.

It should have been a moment of triumph. Only five years before Joni had been a housewife with three children, but no college degree. Teachers loved her because she volunteered for everything, chaperoning field trips, tutoring kids, baking brownies. Yet she wasn't content to be merely a volunteer, an aide, or even a mom. She wanted to be a teacher, herself.

Joni's failing marriage provided the impetus to go back to college. She enrolled full time, and worked nights to pay the bills.

One nightmarish evening she nearly gave up: She had just broken her leg. Her infant son had an ear infection. A major project was due the next morning. There she sat at 1 A.M., her leg propped up, her son asleep on her lap, while her arms reached around him to bang on the typewriter.

Nonetheless, Joni remained on the dean's honor roll nearly every quarter until she finally earned her bachelor's. And now she stood on the threshold of her first classroom—the threshold of a new career. But all she felt was fear.

With good reason. Joni had little actual teaching experience. She would have preferred to be a student teacher, to sit in the back of someone else's class and take notes. However, that was a luxury a now-single woman with three kids couldn't afford. Joni had to earn a paycheck, so she became an "intern" teacher—accepting all the responsibilities of a regular teacher, as well as going to school full time in the evenings. (In addition, of course, to being a full-time mom.)

It was really too much to ask of anyone, and things soon began to unravel. One day Joni intercepted a student's note, which read, "Mrs. G's a bitch!" Another day she lost her temper amid a raucous classroom crayon fight. She cried nearly every day after school. She fell asleep each evening with her books, lesson plans, and papers still strewn around her on the bedspread.

"Things aren't going well," our principal understated at Joni's midterm evaluation.

"I had failed," Joni concurred. "I was devastated because I was so used to succeeding. I had worked so hard, with no results."

Nonetheless, Joni would not despair. She came back from the winter holidays rejuvenated, intent on surviving at least until June. Somehow she did. Barely.

The next September Joni stood again at the door of an empty classroom. "This time, though, I wasn't terrified," she recalled. "I knew what to do—and, more important, what not to do. Above all, I no longer had naive illusions. I knew what was going to walk through my door."

It was a much better year for Joni. "Well, I didn't cry every day."

Perhaps, though, one of her students explained things best in his portfolio: "Mrs. G's made learning fun. . . . Science has become my favorite subject . . . I've enjoyed this quarter and I hope you've seen how successful Mrs. G has been as a teacher to help me learn."

Oh, I'll bet Joni cried when she read that.

Moments of Truth

TERI INVITED ME TO HER ANNUAL PUMPKIN-CARVING PARTY. IT WAS awfully good, yet bittersweet to see her again. You see, we'd gone to graduate school together; but, like most of my friends, she'd soon left education for a job in industry. Her envious questions about my classes, however, betrayed her regrets.

Why did Teri leave? A keen, passionate woman who could not only teach chemistry and physics, but coach volleyball as well—what a wonderful role model she was!

Perhaps it was her schedule. She had pleaded in vain to have her chemistry classes back-to-back in the morning, saving physics for the afternoon. That way she wouldn't have to frantically tear down equipment for experiments and set it back up again many times a day—during her prep period and lunch.

Or perhaps it was the lack of curiosity Teri found in her students. They'd grown accustomed to boring but safe lectures, which required nothing more than mindlessly regurgitating the correct drivel on every exam. Teri, though, made the mistake of expecting her kids to solve problems.

Once, for example, she defined *calorie* as the amount of heat necessary to raise one gram of water one degree centigrade. Then she distributed beakers, thermometers, matches, peanuts, and several other odds and ends. Finally she posed the question: "How many calories are in one peanut?" She gave no further instructions.

Some kids stared dully at the equipment. Others, more daring, carefully measured out a gram of water, plopped the peanut in, and then used the thermometer to see if anything would happen. The A students, however, balked. They angrily demanded Teri tell them what to do. "Think!" she responded in exasperation. Their parents complained to the principal.

I suspect, though, that the worst incident for Teri involved her beloved, electronic balances. After several years of fund-raising and grant-writing, she had procured eight of them—enough for each team of four students in her chemistry class to make incredibly precise measurements.

Unfortunately, the state-of-the-art balances were also perfect for concocting illicit drugs, and one of them mysteriously disappeared. Teri cried.

Three months later, just before graduation, a failing senior met with her after school. "I have a football scholarship to college. I have to pass chemistry!"

"I wish you had been so concerned earlier when I begged you to come for tutoring, to retake quizzes," Teri replied. "I'm afraid now it's too late."

After a moment of silence the youngster whispered, "I could get your balance back. . . ."

Moments of Truth are terrible things. They come upon us unannounced, rarely divulging the right decision. And, in our imperfect world, is the right decision necessarily the best one? How many students might benefit from that missing balance?

Teri gave the boy a D minus.

A less-principled or mediocre teacher might have just recovered the missing balance with a sigh of relief, and moved on. Teri never forgave herself. She quit the following year.

Teaching is difficult, indeed, which is why we need more teachers like Teri. I hope one day she returns.

Be All That You Can Be

MIKE AND I WERE QUITE THE ODD COUPLE IN COLLEGE. HE WAS the battalion commander for the Army ROTC on campus. I was the resident liberal, pinko pacifist. Our friendship seemed absurd, except for the fact that we shared so many classes, exuding in them the same ardent love of philosophy, history, and literature. We both were considering careers in education as well.

Mike usually won our debates. In fact, he once even got me to concede that, in the real world, a national army was a necessary evil; and that, as such, it required officers like him, with both a sharp mind and a warm heart. He taught me a lot.

Mike has since earned the rank of Major, served in Bosnia, and retired. I'm still a teacher, of course—with a bumper sticker on my car proclaiming: "It'll be a great day when our schools have all the money they need, and the Army has to hold a bake sale to buy a tank." (I don't think Mike would approve.)

Why did the Army capture such a talent as Mike, while schools too often cannot?

The answer is simple: The Army made Mike an offer he couldn't refuse. In exchange for a four-year commitment, Uncle Sam picked up all his college expenses. Mike's generals were shrewd, you see. They understood that, in order to recruit the nation's finest college graduates into an all-volunteer army, they'd have to entice them. If Mike is representative of other officers coming out of their ROTC scholarship program, then it's been wildly successful.

Why can't our educational system learn from the Army? (Oh, oh! I just might lose my liberal, pinko card for writing that!) If we hope to similarly lure America's best into our teaching ranks, we're going to have to offer something besides a relatively low salary, and embarrassingly little prestige—especially considering that, in some states, a teaching credential requires an additional year of college. It's no wonder most really talented individuals like Mike—particularly math and science majors—choose other professions.

In times of severe teacher shortages, however, several states have piloted college loan-forgiveness programs to staff their empty classrooms. I suggest we expand these sporadic efforts into a permanent, national campaign, similar to ROTC.

The Army and our schools—like Mike and I—have a lot in common in the end. They're both dedicated to protecting America—the former from our many enemies abroad, the latter from the insidious ones here at home. History will decide which were more dangerous.

In the meantime, I am reminded of another bumper sticker I spied recently: "Do we hate our enemies more than we love our children?" If not, perhaps we ought to recruit our teachers with at least the same vigor as we do our soldiers.

Vindication

THESE ARE TRYING TIMES TO TEACH IN PUBLIC SCHOOLS. SO MANY in government and the media have jumped onto the bash-the-public-schools bandwagon.

Vouchers are the most recent, and the most serious, attack. Implicit in their very existence is the assumption that public schools have failed, and that we educators are to blame. It's a wonder any college graduates at all enter the education profession anymore. It's a wonder so many remain in it.

However, an astounding but little-known piece of research, completed in 1991 by the Sandia National Laboratories, should give teachers heart. (Endless peer-reviews ordered by an apparently disgruntled Bush Administration delayed its dissemination.*)

The Sandia researchers, who had hoped to get to the bottom of "The Problem" with public schools, came to a startling conclusion: "To our surprise, on nearly every measure we found steady or slightly improving trends."

How can this be? Everybody knows that more kids are dropping out than ever before, right?

Wrong. Sandia Labs evaluated graduation figures for the last hundred years and determined that "today's youth are obtaining high school diplomas at unprecedented rates." About 75 percent of our kids graduate on time, and another

---

*For a copy of the Sandia Report, "Perspectives on Education in America," contact Heldref Publications, The Journal of Educational Research, 1319 Eighteenth Street, NW, Washington, DC 20036-1802.

10 percent later go on to obtain a GED. That's the highest rate in our country's history!

Did you know that college graduation figures are even more flattering? At present, one-quarter of our youth garner a college diploma—the highest rate in the world! Even more encouraging is the fact that women and minorities comprise an increasing number and percentage of them.

Ah, but everybody knows that those diplomas don't really mean much anymore. Our standards have fallen. Current SAT scores make that eminently, and depressingly clear.

Wrong again. Sandia Labs found that, while it is true that average SAT scores are lower, this is because elite students aren't the only ones taking the exam anymore. You see, now many, many more kids aspire to college. (Quite an achievement on teachers' part.) Since most of them are from middle and lower classes, it is only natural that average SAT scores have dropped a bit. Nonetheless, the performance of elite kids during the last fifteen years has increased by nearly forty points.

Yeah, but everybody knows that public schools are inefficient, and waste a lot of money. (It's teachers' outlandish salaries, I guess.)

Wrong yet again. Yes, the average per-pupil expenditures have increased dramatically in recent years. But Sandia Labs took the time to look behind those figures. They uncovered that the increase was primarily due to special education classes—the ones for the troubled or learning-disabled kids most private schools refuse to admit. It costs roughly seven times more to teach them.

Once the researchers removed these federally mandated (but unfunded) special education programs from their calculations, they ascertained that the cost of regular public education has remained constant during the past twenty years. In other words, educators have never before done so much with so little.

The Sandia National Laboratories concluded: "The U.S. education system is performing as well as or better than ever before." So, no matter what "everybody knows," educators ought to be mighty proud of themselves.

A Tale of Two Schools

O<small>NCE UPON A TIME THERE WERE TWO SCHOOLS, EACH ON A</small> different side of the tracks.

The first school, Ravenstree High, was on the wrong side. It ministered to poor, minority students. Many of them came from troubled, single-parent families who had never even seen a high school diploma. The kids were only too familiar, though, with gangs and drugs. As a result, Ravenstree's dropout rate was high, its test scores low. Ravenstree wasn't well respected in the community.

It was a shame. The teachers who taught at Ravenstree were among the most dedicated. Many of them had turned down a higher-paying position at more prestigious schools because they wanted to work with disadvantaged kids. They put in long hours calling parents repeatedly, tutoring kids patiently, and planning innovative lessons. Their work paid off. When the Ravenstree's test scores were compared with other wrong-side-of-the-track schools, they were among the highest.

But few in the community ever made that comparison. And so they ridiculed Ravenstree and its teachers.

Meanwhile, the sun was shinning at Palo Blanco High on the other side of the tracks. It had recently been singled out as the best in the state, because it had the highest percentage of kids passing advanced placement tests. Parents—most of them white—took time off from their jobs at the university to attend a special ceremony in the school's monstrous, new theater. The parents saved their loudest applause, though, for the teachers who had somehow managed to help these Stanford/Berkeley-bound kids do well.

The newspapers, of course, covered the gala event. They ran it on their front pages, right next to an article about teenage pregnancies at Ravenstree.

One day, some local politicians became exasperated. "Why can't Ravenstree do as well as Palo Blanco?" they fumed. "The problem is that Ravenstree isn't like a business. It doesn't have to compete with other schools in order to win its students' patronage. Let's give those kids a choice. Then Ravenstree will shape up, or go out of business!"

The community, eager for a quick, painless solution, embraced the idea of school vouchers, or choice.

The following year, about two hundred kids from Ravenstree took their vouchers to Palo Blanco. (Others might have done the same, but they couldn't afford the cost of the daily crosstown transportation.)

Of the two hundred, Palo Blanco accepted only thirty. (Coincidentally, they turned out to be either the brightest students or the fastest athletes.) Still, despite the numerous applicants, Palo Blanco made no plans to build more classrooms. The addition of so many kids from Ravenstree might "upset the warm, homogeneous atmosphere of the place," explained Palo Blanco's smiling principal.

Meanwhile, Ravenstree's principal wasn't smiling. She began the year with thirty fewer student leaders, and a lot less state funding. Most of her students had really never had a choice, and now they were left with even less.

Only one of the schools lived happily ever after.

Rest Easy

I JUST WANTED TO REASSURE EVERYONE THAT, DURING THESE TENSE weeks of testing in schools (SAT 9), everything is OK.

For instance, obedient to State Department of Education requirements, I have removed the large map in the back of my classroom, and covered up with sheets anything else on the walls that might give my students some sort of advantage on the exam. Every one of my colleagues and I sat through a video admonishing us against adding or deleting a single word from the instructions we'll read to students. Also, we've signed affidavits pledging we will not copy or even discuss any part of the test. Just in case, though, administrators keep it under lock and key until just moments before testing begins each day; and they collect it and all peripheral materials again immediately afterwards. They'll confiscate every scrap of scratch paper my students use, as well, so that it can be sent off to SAT 9 head-quarters for analysis and evaluation.

Even Heaven can't help the teacher or school less scrupulous with these meticulous precautions. In fact, one, small misstep could result in the invalidation of the entire district's scores.

I know all this will come as a relief to you. Given the tremendous disparities between and among California's schools, you might worry that some students could have an unfair advantage over others during testing.

Indeed, last May the ACLU sued the State Department of Education for providing so many children—who just happen to be predominately poor and minority—an awful education. The ACLU cited inner-city schools, for example, where dead rats slowly decompose in the corners of gymnasiums; and where those rats' living brethren brazenly wander the halls during school hours; where bathrooms, if they work at all (don't even ask about the water fountains), reek of urine and worse; where technology is nonexistent and teachers lack even a single class-set of textbooks.

Of course, those teachers represent the most pathetic and glaring form of educational injustice. Recent research has revealed teachers to be the single most important factor in determining a student's success or failure. In fact, teacher quality is more important than even class size and a child's socio-economic status.

Nonetheless, California's best teachers rarely staff those dilapidated, inner-city schools. No, a disproportionate number of teachers there possess only emergency credentials. Worse, at some schools the annual teacher-turnover rate exceeds 60 percent—with, of course, dire implications for the education of their students.

It is understandable, then, with the obvious disinterest the State of California has displayed in acknowledging, much less addressing the outrageous disparities in the learning environments of its children, you might worry the same could be true with their testing environments. As I noted before, however, education officials are apparently obsessed with ensuring all students are tested the same.

This is crucial, you know, since accurate SAT 9 test results will reveal how—surprise, surprise—at too many inner-city schools, children learn virtually nothing. Thus, it'll be easier than ever to ridicule such children, belittle their teachers, despair in public education, and argue for vouchers.

So, never fear: The Department of Education is doing everything in its power to make sure that, at least during testing, all schools are equal. We can all rest easy. I know I will.

Noble, Naive Ideals

CHRIS AND I HAD SO MUCH IN COMMON IN GRAD SCHOOL, especially our idealism. We resolved to teach children who were the most in need of a good education. So, although we both might have worked in affluent, prestigious school districts, we spurned them. Chris went off to inner-city Los Angeles, and I to Union City, south of Oakland. Then we lost touch with each other.

I often wondered why I never called Chris. I rationalized it by telling myself I was simply too busy; and I'd be in L.A. one of these weekends, anyway. I'd see him then.

I never went, though. I never wrote. I never called.

Eventually I had to acknowledge the nagging reason why. It was a TV news report after the Rodney King riots that shook me up. The account highlighted an inner-city classroom in L.A. where children were only barely able to contain their trauma and fear. Their eyes bled tears of anguish. Their voices cracked with despair.

I immediately recalled Chris, and that those students might be his. And I felt ashamed. Just the day before I'd written an article about my school, congratulating it for remaining "an oasis in the turbulent lives of my students . . . a place where kids can be safe, love each other, and hope in the future." Chris couldn't say the same about his school. Why wasn't I there at his side?

Of course, teaching in Union City was no cakewalk. Speaking twenty-two different languages, more than a third of my students were poor enough to participate in the federal lunch program. Too many of them came from families beset by alcoholism and ignorance. My friends back in Ohio thought I was some kind of martyr for teaching them. And I must admit to a certain amount of pride in the fact that I did help children much less fortunate than I.

Yet, whenever I'd thought of Chris, I'd wondered if I had betrayed our commitment of so long ago. My challenges were minor compared to what he faced every day in L.A. Most likely, all of his students were poor. His classroom would be run down, overcrowded, and underequipped. His school wasn't an oasis, but a jungle where gangs stalked the halls.

I'd always admired Chris for entering that frightening jungle, but I hadn't dared go myself. I was no Jaime Escalante. Heck, I'd often felt overwhelmed even in peaceful Union City. I could succeed, though, at least with most of my students. The situation wasn't hopeless. I wasn't so sure about Los Angeles. I doubted I could survive there.

As it turned out, neither could Chris. After the news report, I finally called a mutual friend to find out how Chris was doing, and how I could get back in touch with him. Our friend informed me that Chris had cared too much, struggled too hard. Four months before he'd suffered a nervous breakdown, and left teaching.

Chris and I had vowed to save the poorest of the poor. In the end, I'd been afraid to try. Chris had tried, but failed. What happened to our noble, naive ideals? What will happen to all those unfortunate kids we abandoned?

One Size Doesn't Fit All

THERE IS ONLY ONE JAIME ESCALANTE. HE BECAME THE MOST famous teacher in America in 1987 when the film *Stand and Deliver* recounted his unparalleled achievement. He'd left his lucrative high-tech career to instruct math at Garfield High School in East Los Angeles. With nothing more than his dynamic personality, his unconventional pedagogy, and his dogged belief that "students will rise to the level of our expectations," he eventually motivated 60 percent of his apparently disadvantaged students—more than 140 kids a year!—to pass the demanding Advanced Placement Calculus exam. Escalante thus became an inspiration for teachers everywhere, including me.

Nonetheless, his astounding success cannot be easily replicated.

You see, the Escalante miracle was almost totally dependent on him and his singular gifts. It's the same with other prodigies. No one, for example, would argue that, if only every quarterback imitated Joe Montana, they too would win Super Bowls. Or that, if only more singers drank, smoked, and wore hats, they'd become the next Frank Sinatra. Similarly, there is no "Escalante" Calculus manual or step-by-step "stand and deliver" teaching method. There is only one Jaime Escalante.

Also, it should be noted that Escalante forsook everything for his students. His marriage languished. His own children struggled in school. He himself suffered a heart attack. Surely school boards cannot expect the same of all teachers!

What, then, are the rest of us poor mortal educators, who possess neither Escalante's genius nor his fanaticism, supposed to do? We can admire. We can imitate. But we cannot duplicate. There is only one Jaime Escalante.

And, that is as it should be. Teaching is an art, after all. We educators don't create widgets that are all the same shape and size. We nurture, guide, and ultimately love children, each and every one of them a distinct creation, each with a unique personality, culture, and learning style. What works with one child may be disastrous for another.

Unfortunately, Escalante himself demonstrated this. Even he couldn't find success in his new school, Hiram Johnson High. There he no longer taught calculus because only six students signed up for the course. At least a third of his algebra students dropped out of his class. And he received a poor professional evaluation. Apparently his bantering style, where he alternately ridicules then praises ("What are you, some stupid kid?"), didn't play as well in Sacramento as it had in East L.A.

So, there is an important lesson to Escalante's legacy: Beware of any attempt to legislate, mandate, or codify the best way to teach calculus, English, or anything else. Children and education are too complex for that. In fact, standardization succeeds only in driving away artists such as Escalante, and ensuring that everyone is equally mediocre.

None of this diminishes Escalante. If anything, he is to be admired even more for refusing to rest on his laurels, or to ride off into a sunset. No, unlike movies, in real life the sun inevitably rises the next morning, and heroes must once again ride courageously out to face yet another dragon, knowing that this time they may not win. That's what Escalante did.

But, of course, there is only one Jaime Escalante.

Momentous Moment

BILLY'S COUNSELOR HAD WARNED ME ABOUT HIM. SHE'D TOLD me he was "school-phobic," and likely to be an attendance problem.

I decided right then, before I had even met him, that I liked him. You see, I'd been just like Billy in eighth grade. I, too, had been unusually short and apparently uncoordinated. I knew very well what it was like to be at the bottom of the all-important social scale, to be ridiculed constantly and cruelly for no reason. I'd hated school almost as much as Billy did. How could I help but like him?

I wished I could have shared what I finally learned, many years after middle school. But some things—such as the ability to like yourself, and the courage to strive for more—cannot be taught. Billy would have to discover them for himself. The miracle was that he did, right before my eyes.

Billy probably doesn't remember the day he began, though. He was working with three other students on a cooperative team project about Manifest Destiny. Each student had taken one part of the project (I think Billy was responsible for Texas) and had become an expert on it. On that day, all would share what they had learned with the other members of the team.

I liked the Manifest Destiny project a lot. It forced kids to rely on and be accountable to each other. Such positive peer pressure usually motivated most to work harder. In Billy's case, I'd hoped it would encourage him to just show up. The question was, which would he fear more—teaching some of the kids who made fun of him, or having to explain his absence to them after he'd let them down?

Well, Billy did finally slink into the classroom that fateful day, just before the bell. Dreading what lay ahead, he nonetheless dragged his desk into the team's circle. Mercifully, two of his teammates preceded him, so he could spend the first thirty minutes simply taking notes. Finally, Billy's turn came. I stood off in the corner and watched.

Billy began teaching slowly, tentatively. He kept his eyes glued to his notes. His voice was soft and timid. This time, however, he faced no twisted smirks, but sincere questions. After all, only he had the answers. His teammates needed him.

With each point Billy made, he gained momentum and confidence. Once he even ventured a joke, and everybody laughed—with him, not at him. That was all he needed. Soon he was out of his desk, scurrying around the team, eagerly checking other students' notes. "No, no. You still don't understand," he said. "Listen this time, and I'll explain it again." When the period ended, Billy actually groaned. For the first time in a long while, he had enjoyed himself at school.

I returned the graded projects the following week. Billy's team had earned an A minus. One of his team members turned to him, slapped him five, and said, "Yes! We did it!" I don't think Billy missed another day of school.

A year later, the counselor and I went to see Billy perform in his first high school play, *Oklahoma*. We gave him a standing ovation. "I was only in the chorus," he remarked sheepishly afterwards. Only? Someday, perhaps, Billy will understand how very momentous that performance was.

No Fear

DANIEL APPEARED AT MY CLASSROOM DOOR ONE MORNING, nonchalantly handing me the notice adding him to my class. He was not like most students. It wasn't just his deep, mature voice, which seemed to belie his diminutive stature. Maybe it was his aloof demeanor, for, while pleasant and personable, he manifest neither interest nor respect. It seemed as if my class and I were irrelevant to him, as if he had his heart set on something, somewhere else.

Sure enough, less than two weeks later Daniel disappeared. "He ran away from his foster home," the counselor informed me. "He's gone."

Where? Why? My curiosity haunted me until, finally, I sat across from Marilyn. For fifteen years she had operated the halfway house where Daniel briefly stayed.

Marilyn, too, remarked on Daniel's uniqueness. "His smile, strangely enough, seemed to go from his lips to his eyes. It came from within. He had a positive personality, and seemed willing to work on his problems. That's why I agreed to take him in with the other boys."

She shook her head and sighed. "But then I noticed how he spent so much time alone every evening on the balcony off his bedroom, just staring out over the Bay. He was mesmerized by the lights, by the BART trains. I knew he longed to return to his gang. He just couldn't handle a lack of chaos."

I didn't understand. "Daniel's spent most of his life on the streets," Marilyn explained. "He's been with his gang since he was six years old." Then, in response to my incredulity, she added, "Dave, a child, no matter how young, is going to try to meet its needs. For whatever reason, Daniel never had a real family with his parents. But he found one with the gang."

Daniel had stayed out most evenings with the gang until the early hours of the morning. Sometimes he wouldn't return home at all, sleeping instead in an abandoned building the gang had taken over. He'd sold marijuana to make money. Finally he'd been arrested trying to steal a car. After a month in Juvenile Hall, he had been sent to Marilyn's halfway house, and my class.

"Daniel was such a needy child," Marilyn reflected. "He so desperately needed a normal setting. But in the end, he couldn't tolerate it."

I recalled with a shudder the million or so street kids of San Paulo, Brazil. Wild, apparently uneducable, only a few could endure the transition to normal society, even when the most benevolent person or agency tried to guide them. Most wound up on the streets again. Was Daniel like that? (Maybe he wasn't so unique after all.)

Marilyn sat thoughtfully for a moment or so, and then nodded her head. "Perhaps, the problem with Daniel is he has no thought for the future, no planning. He lives only for the moment. You see, nice as he is, Daniel has no fear."

I gazed out at the lights of the Bay that had so beckoned Daniel. I thought of him roving with his gang among them all night. And, unlike Daniel, I was very afraid, indeed.

Wimp

JAY COULDN'T WAIT FOR BASKETBALL TRYOUTS. I DREADED THEM.

During the two weeks prior to the fateful day, he'd dash up to me almost every recess, his knee-length plaid, cotton shirt (the rage that year) billowing behind him. Out of breath, he'd just grin for a few moments, and then begin his litany of eager questions: When were the tryouts again? How many days would they last? How many kids would make the team? What should he wear?

Jay quickly endeared himself to me. While most students hid behind a stolid facade, he exuded unabashed enthusiasm. His grin proved infectious, and soon I was almost as anxious as he for tryouts to begin.

However, as more and more kids signed up, my own grin became smaller and smaller. I had only twelve uniforms, so most of those trying out wouldn't make the team. Jay was one of the shortest kids on the list. What if I had to cut him? Why, I'd break his heart—and mine.

The first day of tryouts, forty-two kids ran through the various drills along with Jay. I was ruthless. I looked for any excuse to cross names off the list, and I didn't play favorites. One too many botched layups, or a little slow on the sprints, and my merciless pen fell. When the carnage was over, only eighteen names remained.

Early the following morning, I posted the call-back list outside my classroom door. Within seconds it was mobbed. I couldn't bear to watch, and retreated cowardly inside. I heard some shouts of joy, and imagined the painful silences of those who didn't find their names on the list. They'd force a smile, pretend they didn't care, and then wander off, pursued by the inevitable, cruel taunts from those who hadn't had the courage to tryout themselves: "Ah-ha, Nick! You didn't even make it past the first day!" I hate tryouts.

A few moments later, Jay poked his head inside the room. "I'll see you again this afternoon, Mr. Ellison!" he cried in glee. He had survived the first cuts.

That afternoon, Jay and the rest of the remaining hopefuls scrimmaged each other while I watched, making cryptic marks on my clipboard, ranking each player according to how much he could offer the team. Only the top twelve would make it. An hour later, I was finished. Jay was ranked fourteenth.

Afterward, as the kids retrieved their books in my class-room, many pestered me for some clue. "How'd I do, Mr. Ellison?"

Once again the coward, I just shook my head and said, "Check the list tomorrow."

One by one, the kids went home, until only Jay remained. He sat, motionless and silent in the back of the room. His usual grin was gone. He knew. He wanted to beg, to plead, to tell me how hard he'd try. But he couldn't speak. He couldn't even look at me. Finally, he left.

Well, I'm a wimp. I put fourteen names on that final list. I had to borrow two mismatched soccer uniforms. And I knew that, with such a large team (and my insistence on playing everyone at least a quarter), I'd lose a few games I wouldn't have otherwise.

I also knew I didn't have the heart to cut Jay.

The Karate Kid

STEVE FULFILLED A FANTASY OF MINE. YOU SEE, UNLIKE HIM, I'D been a puny eighth grader, the scrawny kid the bullies loved to pick on. I always imagined that one day I would learn Jujitsu or Karate, and take my revenge.

More recently I'd fantasized that a monster of a student, such as a huge football player, would advance on me in class, backing me into a corner. With the rest of my students staring wide-eyed, I would vanquish him with a single "Hai-ya!" and he would crumple to the floor. Of course, the best part would be the looks of awe I would enjoy afterwards as I walked through the halls. I never imagined, though, that the monster would be as nice as Steve.

I came to know Steve because two of my students were his only friends. Often the three of them would harass me during recess in a good-natured, junior-high sort of way. They traded bald jokes, each one trying to outdo the other. "Oh, Mr. Ellison, please wear a hat! The glare off your head is blinding me!" Steve, on the other hand, stayed with one, consistent prank. Towering above me, he mimicked the sound of spitting, and then pantomimed the motions of buffing and shining the top of my head. I feigned impatience with it all. But, to be honest, Steve and his friends made me laugh.

One day when Steve came to my classroom, however, I needed to talk with his two friends privately about some missing work. I asked him to wait outside. On his way out, he attacked another student, whom he would have pummeled to pieces had I not intervened. I grabbed Steve in a bear hug, pinning his arms. Nonetheless, he continued to struggle hysterically. I finally just fell to the floor, bringing him with me. Stunned, he lay there motionless until the assistant principal arrived.

Only after I spoke to the counselor did I understand what had happened. For the past several months Steve's mother had abandoned Steve for her new boyfriend. She no longer cooked or cleaned for him. In fact, she seemed to have completely forgotten about him, leaving him alone to raise himself. I could imagine the rejection and the anger he must have felt. Then, when I appeared to exclude him from his only friends, he snapped. He lashed out at the first student who looked at him the wrong way.

Later I saw Steve crying alone in the assistant principal's office. He wasn't the monster of my fantasy. He was merely a confused, hurt, lonely boy.

On my way back to class, many students gathered around me to ask, "Is it true you slammed Steve?" News of a fight travels fast in a middle school. Even the gym teacher clenched his fist as I passed, and saluted me with a new nickname, "Hammer Man!" How often had I wished for just such a reputation? Now I couldn't stand it, knowing I had earned it at Steve's expense.

I forbade anyone to use the nickname or to even mention the fight. And I waited anxiously for Steve's return, hoping against hope he'd still want to give my head a buff and a shine.

Magic

WHEN I DO A FAVOR FOR MY STUDENTS, OR CUT THEM A BREAK, I often ask, "Now, who's your favorite teacher?" I'm hoping that such bribery will induce the kids to flatter me. I usually succeed—except when the students are members of the band. Then they invariably respond in unison, "Mr. D.C., of course!" It's maddening.

One year D.C. invited me to accompany his band on its trip to Disneyland. I jumped at the chance, not only because I knew I'd have a great time, but because I hoped to discover his secret. Well, I did. He uses magic.

How else can I explain what happened our first night? One hundred and seventeen seventh and eighth graders lay strewn in their sleeping bags on the National Guard Armory's floor. Many of them had never slept away from home before and could barely contain their excitement. I expected an hour or more of hoots, giggles, and the inevitable farts before the kids, finally exhausted, fell asleep.

Not D.C. With a mischievous wink at me, he blew his whistle and announced that, if the kids didn't go to sleep immediately, he'd conduct a marching practice right then and there. Fifteen seconds later silence prevailed. Soon, everyone slept. Magic!

There was no rest for D.C., though. He unloaded the wayward instrument truck, finalized the list of parent chaperones, arranged the kids' "Disney Dollars," and took care of the sundry other details necessary for us all to enjoy ourselves the next day. Finally, at about four A.M., he crawled into his own sleeping bag. Forty-five minutes later, the first kids awoke. And D.C. greeted them with his usual wacky humor.

The next afternoon, the students eagerly donned their flashy, new uniforms. (The booster club D.C. had organized had sewn most of them the year before.) Then they scampered into place for a final practice, their mirrored sunglasses reflecting D.C.'s image back at him, pacing before them. He had ensured that the kids looked great. Now he'd make sure they sounded even better.

For the umpteen thousandth time he led the kids through the music he had written for them—a medley of Disney tunes, each song a different, challenging style.

"Brass" he screamed, "don't blat it out! Just touch it! Blend!" And, of course, they did. They were ready.

When D.C. had first come to Barnard, the band, half as small, had been the scourge of the district. That weekend, though, beneath a radiant sun, the Barnard-White Middle School Marching Band paraded proudly down Main Street in Disneyland. One of the thousands of spectators asked, "Where's that high school from?"

Magic is the only explanation. It's a magic born of uncommon skill, an impossible dream, dedication bordering on madness, and, above all, boundless love. D.C.'s students recognized that love. That's why they'd play anything for him, march anywhere with him.

At the end of the year, one of D.C.'s musicians came in to my classroom crying. An eighth grader, she had just turned in her uniform. It wasn't the uniform she'd miss. It was D.C., and his magic.

Sad Burden

THERE ARE FEW THINGS AS DISTURBING AS MEETING A CHILD LIKE Susan who, although only thirteen, is profoundly unhappy.

With a movie star's face and a figure to match, she might have been pretty. However, her perpetual frown and her icy cynicism overwhelmed any potential beauty. Her misery was plain for all to see. While I strove to create a jovial classroom atmosphere, she seemed to always find a way to bitterly disagree with just about everyone, especially me.

I tried to talk with Susan several times, but she kept whatever troubled her carefully hidden, perhaps even from herself.

One day in class, Susan unexpectedly offered a glimpse of what was the matter. We were about to read a short story about an eccentric, old-fashioned gentleman. In preparation, everyone had written a brief journal entry describing some acquaintance who just didn't understand or agree with modern times. I asked Susan to be the first to share her thoughts.

She hesitated for a long moment, indecisive. Then she plunged headlong into an emotional reading of her journal entry: "My father doesn't understand me, or anyone. He doesn't because he thinks only about himself. He's the most selfish person I know. . . . I hate him!"

Everyone stared at Susan, aghast. As I could think of no adequate response (I certainly didn't want to pursue a public discussion of her father), I hastily thanked her for sharing, then asked someone else to read from his journal. Perhaps I erred, for when I tried to speak with Susan afterwards, it was too late.

The window to her tortured soul had closed again. She would share no more.

I knew Susan came from a broken family, and that the divorce had been a messy one. Did she blame her father? Had he abused her, physically or sexually? That would explain her hostility toward me, another male adult. I could only guess, and wonder.

Several weeks later, Susan's inner torments erupted in class once again. We were discussing the dangers of alcohol during Red Ribbon Week. I was explaining the genetic factor involved in alcoholism, that the tendency to abuse alcohol might run in the family.

Susan interrupted with an explosive outburst. "That's not true, Mr. Ellison! My grandfather, my father, and my aunt are all alcoholics. But I'm not! You don't know what you're talking about!"

This time, however, I think I said the right thing. I began by agreeing that she was not predestined to be an alcoholic. "Just as I'm not, Susan. My grandfather too was an alcoholic." I also acknowledged that I sometimes didn't know what I was talking about. "The only thing I know for sure," I added, "is that we all have to learn to deal with our problems openly and honestly. Then we can avoid alcoholism, or addiction to any other drug." My words seemed to mollify her. Yet, as before, she wasn't interested in continuing the discussion later.

I never found out the relationship between alcoholism and Susan's professed hatred for her dad. She went off to high school, taking her mysterious, sad burden with her.

Every year, though, during Red Ribbon Week, I remember her. I recall that drugs and alcohol can maim kids, even if the kids themselves never abuse them. And I renew my prayer that someday Susan will find peace, and some measure of joy.

Red Ribbon Dialogues

Dear Parents,

Red Ribbon Week always makes me impatient with you. For example, this year I worked with some of your eighth-grade children on writing "Red Ribbon Conversations." We had been learning to punctuate dialogues anyway, so it was only natural that we use the newly refined skill to practice "just saying no."

My students were to pretend that they were at some party where there were drugs such as alcohol. They had to imagine what kind of peer pressure they would face, and how they would deal with it. I even gave them permission to, if necessary, tell some little white lies.

Some of your children were quite creative with their fibbing. "Oh, I'd love a beer," one wrote, "but I'm taking some prescription anti-zit medication. I'll just have a soda."

Others had the courage (easy in an essay for school!) to simply refuse outright: "For the third time, no! And if you call me a nerd again, I'm leaving!"

"Very good!" I encouraged my students, smiling and nodding my head. But inside I was seething. You see, it occurred to me that what I was really trying to protect them from was the negligence of you, their parents.

I ask you, Why should I have to prepare your young children for such adult situations and choices? Put more plainly, Why do you allow your kids to attend parties where there's alcohol? Really, it's you parents who must learn to "just say no."

How many of you blissfully send your kids off to a party each weekend, assuming that someone else will ensure that it is safe, and alcohol-free? And, then, when your children get in a fight, drive drunk, become pregnant, get AIDS, you ask helplessly, "What's wrong with our schools?"

Frankly, I'm tired of it.

So, I have some Red Ribbon homework for you, too. It's due this Friday, just in time for the weekend:

> Pretend your teenager has just asked to go to a party. Write the ensuing dialogue. In it, be sure to include many more questions than simply, "What time will you be home?" You must practice strategies to determine the last names of your child's friends, the telephone number of their parents, the address and telephone number of the party, and the *names* (emphasis on the plural) of the chaperones.
>
> Then, imagine the tremendous pressure you'll face from your child—remarks such as, "Oh, you're so out-of-it!" or "All the other parents are letting their kids go!"—and how you'll respond.
>
> Lastly, make sure you include the line, "No, you may not go." Believe me, it'll be a lot easier on paper than in real life; but that's why you need to practice.
>
> For extra credit, list three alternative evening activities for your children, which you could both organize and chaperone.

Remember, parents: Education begins at home. And Red Ribbon Week must begin there too.

Parents "No" Best

MY PARENTS HAD THE COURAGE TO SAY "NO" WHEN I WAS growing up. At the time I didn't understand. I pouted. I screamed. I ranted and raved. "I'll be the laughing stock at school!" But they remained firm: "No!"

Buying shoes was never an exciting excursion in the Ellison family, for example, because we always got the same style, Dexter saddle shoes. ("Army-surplus clod-stompers," I called them.) Oh, how I longed for a pair of penny-loafers! Then I would be able to strut in style! But, "No!" my mom said. The Dexters were eminently practical, their soles lasting a full year, sometimes two. And that was that. Who ever had parents as unreasonable as mine?

The hand-me-down clothes they gave me weren't any better. I can't describe my utter humiliation when my teachers would compliment them. "Why, Dave, I remember that beautiful sweater on your oldest brother, Kevin." Aaagh!

The worst, though, were the trips to the barbershop. As quickly as the barber could switch on his electric razor (no need for scissors or a comb!) most of my hair would be gone.

"Haircuts are too expensive," Dad lamented. "We don't want to have to come back here next month because your hair has already grown out."

Easy for him to say! He didn't have to endure the tauntings I did the next morning: "Peach-Fuz! Watermelon!" At times I hated my parents.

Now that I am a teacher, though, I appreciate their stubbornness. You see, every day I have to deal with kids whose parents haven't learned to say "No." The results are alternately comical and sad, and sometimes even frightening.

Many of my boys, for example, simply must have their hair cut every few weeks or so in order to keep their "racing stripes" razor sharp. Likewise, too many of my girls fail P.E. because they refuse to dress for class. It seems that running or changing into T-shirts might mess-up their hair. I'm not kidding. And the craziest thing is that their parents allow them to continue failing, year after year!

Many parents now spend more than a hundred dollars just for a pair of high-tech "pump-up" basketball shoes—often for kids who get winded just jogging to the cafeteria. I'm afraid to ask how much parents invest in the sport team jackets so many of my students wear, even on the hottest of days.

As I watch the poor kids sweating in agony—but smiling smugly in the knowledge that they are in style—I realize that my parents accomplished a lot more than simply save money with all their "Nos." They communicated to me—subtly but emphatically—that impressing people with what I wore would not be a priority for me. Preparing myself for college would be. They later lavishly spent every dime they had saved on my college education.

My mom and dad freed me from the tyranny of style. They taught me to have the courage to be myself, and to struggle to make of myself somebody great. By denying me so much, they gave me what mattered most.

Saint Washington

MANY OF THE SIMPLE TRUTHS MY MOM TAUGHT ME I PASS ON TO my students.

I remember, for example, one suggestion she made when I was twelve years old. I went to Catholic school, and had to choose a saint for my confirmation name. St. Philip? St. James? I couldn't decide.

"Choose St. Peter," she said. "He was always screwing up!"

I gave her a hurt look.

"Relax, Dave," she laughed, "and listen. Peter was often vain and selfish. He even lied three times and betrayed Jesus. Nonetheless, Jesus chose him to lead His church. Now, there's a saint you can believe in. St. Peter was human, Dave, just like you. So if he could become a saint, you can too."

I recall that advice every Presidents' Day. My teachers taught me that Washington was perfect: He never told a lie, made fools out of the British, and single-handedly founded our nation. Hail, St. Washington! But who could ever aspire to be as wonderful as he?

Because of my mom, I paint a more human (and more realistic) portrait of Washington for my students. I tell them that, like St. Peter, Washington made a few serious mistakes along the way:

> In 1754, Washington was a young, brash surveyor. He was supposed to lead a small detachment into the wilderness and discourage the French from building forts there. Washington

arrived too late, though. The French already manned their forts, and vastly outnumbered Washington's force. They sent an ambassador to discuss things with Washington, and so turn him back peaceably.

The ambassador never had a chance. Eager for glory, Washington attacked the ambassador's party and killed everyone. Thus began the French and Indian War, which soon escalated into a world war. Oops!

The French easily captured Washington, and released him only because they couldn't take such a foolish, young man seriously. If only they had known!

About twenty-five years later, Washington was the victor, having defeated the British in the American Revolution. Thanks, ironically, to the help of the French! It was French strategy and French cannons that forced the British to surrender at Yorktown.

Nonetheless, Washington's officers were not celebrating. They had not been paid. They wanted to march on Philadelphia, disband the Continental Congress, and establish military rule. They would receive their pay, by God!

Only one man could stop them. Washington. He knew that everything they did would set a long-lasting precedent. A military coup would lead the new country down a violent path away from democracy. (The French later took that path.) Washington pleaded with his officers to be patient, to trust him. In the end, they did—not because he was a great general (he *wasn't*), but because he was simply a great human being whom they respected and loved.

The officers never did receive their pay. But neither did their descendants receive the ugly legacy of military dictatorship. We all owe that—and much, much more—to Washington.

I tell my students Washington is a hero they can believe in. Yes, he really screwed up. But he went on to do great things. So can they, I tell them. Just as my mom told me.

All Equal?

"I HATE HISTORY!" ANGELA SAID ONE DAY IN CLASS. WE WERE trying to make some sense out of the Declaration of Independence, and somewhere between "When in the course of human events . . ." and ". . . our sacred honor" she had become exasperated. "Who cares what a dead man wrote two hundred years ago anyway? Why do we waste our time studying this?"

I had considered my usual cop-out, that "those who don't know history are doomed to repeat it," but such an obtuse answer would never satisfy Angela, or Thomas Jefferson. Besides, it suddenly occurred to me that the Declaration of Independence itself provided a particularly powerful argument, not only for studying history, but for education in general.

"Angela," I responded after a moment to gather my thoughts, "two hundred years ago, most everyone would have agreed with you. Why should you waste your time on any of this? After all, they'd say, you're just an ignorant Hispanic woman. We'd better leave history for a few, select, white men who can comprehend and appreciate it. You need to know only enough to obey them. Yep, Angela, you're right. Close your text. You're wasting your time."

She refused. "I am not ignorant!" she responded indignantly.

"Oh, so you agree with Thomas Jefferson, then?"

"What?"

"Well, before the Age of Enlightenment, people believed that most citizens were pretty stupid. They thought they needed a king to make the important decisions for them. But Thomas

Jefferson disagreed. In this document, he expressed the notion that average citizens, provided they were well educated, could decide for themselves. That's what he meant by 'All men are created equal.' Do you agree, then, with Jefferson's Declaration, Angela? Are you the equal of any king?"

"Heck yeah!" she insisted.

"Well, beware then. For there are many out there who are anxious for you to fail, and to prove that a Hispanic woman cannot be trusted with responsibility or authority. It's just like two hundred years ago when many in Europe took bets on how long the United States—a nation ruled by peasant farmers—would survive. They expected anarchy."

"Well, we proved them wrong," Angela answered smugly.

"Really? Remember, Angela, Jefferson's experiment isn't over."

"What do you mean?"

"I mean most Americans don't even vote. And when we ask those few who do about the issues or the candidates, nearly half reveal they have no idea what they're voting for. As a result, our government is beset by corruption and mismanagement. Of course, this is not even to mention the fact that a Hispanic woman has yet to become president."

She was silent.

"Angela, it's one thing to declare our independence, to claim that all men and women are equal, and that we can be trusted to govern ourselves. It's another thing to prove it. We're a long way from accomplishing that.

"That's why we study Jefferson's declaration, Angela. To learn that the idea of real democracy was—and is—a risky experiment. It's up to us—up to you, Angela—to make sure it succeeds."

Salutary Neglect

ONCE UPON A TIME THERE WERE TWO HIGH SCHOOL FRESHMEN named Susan and Elizabeth. They were the best of friends, even though they had starkly distinct personalities.

Susan had been raised by liberal parents who trusted her, allowed her to do whatever she pleased. If she wanted to stay out late with friends, she just called home and let her folks know where she was. She attended all the parties and dances. She'd developed a confident, charming personality.

Elizabeth, however, was demure, perhaps even a bit sad. You see, she had parents from the Old School who had rarely permitted her to do anything fun. She'd never gone on a date with a boy, and always, always had to be home by ten P.M., even on weekends. She seemed stoically resigned to her, thus cloistered, fate.

One bright day, two strapping older boys—football players both—asked Susan and Elizabeth to go to the upcoming homecoming dance. This was quite an honor, and the two girls hugged each other gleefully, squealing in delight. Then Elizabeth abruptly stopped and collapsed on a bench in tears. "Oh, who am I fooling?" she sobbed. "My parents will never let me go. Never!" Susan, too, was upset. She realized she'd probably have to go to homecoming without her friend.

Sure enough, Elizabeth's parents shook their heads sternly at the news. Susan's parents, though, were uncharacteristically taken aback. They excused themselves for a private chat. When they returned, they said, "Susan, Honey, we know we've always let you do whatever you wanted. But these are older boys, and there'll likely be alcohol at the party afterwards. We're really sorry, but we think you ought to wait a year or two. There will be other homecomings, other boys. . . ."

So, as it turned out, neither Elizabeth nor Susan could go. The next day, one of them ran away from home. Which one do you suppose it was?

I used to tell this tale every year in my eighth-grade U.S. History class. (I'd stolen the story from one of my graduate school professors.) There is no correct answer, of course. The important thing is that my students all found the story interesting. It involved them, at least indirectly. They could all identify with one of the girls, or compare their parents with Susan's or Elizabeth's.

Thus, when I finally introduced the concept of Salutary Neglect, I would simply state, "In the years prior to the American Revolution, the Thirteen Colonies were like Susan." My students could infer the rest: The colonies were accustomed to doing pretty much whatever they pleased. But after the French and Indian War, Mother England, now broke, clamped down and, as in The Proclamation of 1763, began to say "No." The colonies threw a temper tantrum of sorts, and eventually ran away.

The American Revolution was a lot more complicated than that, of course; but the story of Susan and Elizabeth is a wonderful introduction, one which my students long remembered, and even made reference to in their later essays.

As the adage goes, "Tell me, and I forget. Show me, and I remember. Involve me, and I understand."

Proud, But Wary

"HOW LONG WILL I BE UNDER ARREST?"

Jorge, the chief immigration official in the tiny, muddy village lost in the Lacondan Jungle, merely shrugged his shoulders.

"Hey, you have to at least inform the United States Embassy. I have my rights!"

"You're in Mexico now," Jorge responded flatly.

It was July of 1984, during my most angry phase of anti-Americanism. Bloody civil wars raged in Central America, the inevitable result of injustices and atrocities committed by ruthless American-sponsored dictators. I'd screamed at rallies, carried placards in front of federal buildings, written letters to newspapers. . . . Nonetheless, most everyone remained apathetic. They dismissed my rantings as exaggerations or lies.

So, I'd trekked to Boca LaCantun, a refugee camp just north of the Mexican border with Guatemala. I'd help out as I could, and document, myself, the Guatemalan Indians' reports of the genocide occurring just across the border.

Or, so I'd hoped. As soon as I had arrived I'd been arrested, strip-searched, and interrogated.

Two days later the "Federales" arrived. Wearing no uniforms, but sporting M16 assault rifles, they frightened even Jorge. It soon became apparent that they protected the drug trade, which flourished in this remote jungle. And they knew that I knew, which is why they decided to kill me.

Jorge saved my life. In the middle of the night, during a torrential downpour, he stealthily whisked me out of camp and drove me in his jeep north to Palenque. He frantically arranged to have lots of people meet me. "The more who know of you, the harder it is to disappear you," he explained.

A week later I was "safe" in prison in Mexico City. There the guards used DDT to control the lice, fleas, and bedbugs. Other times they tortured many of my fellow inmates. Guatemalans fared the worst.

There was, however, one American couple who'd already spent six weeks behind bars. Their crime? They'd been robbed, and later had stumbled on the thief. Unfortunately, when he'd bribed the police, they'd thrown a fit, so the police arrested them instead. Like all good Ugly Americans, they were still raising hell, which explained, I suspected, why they languished in prison.

Thanks to my ingratiating behavior, and to one kind-hearted prisoner who, upon his release, informed the United States Embassy of my whereabouts, I was deported only two weeks later. I'd never been informed of the charges against me. I'd never spoken to a lawyer. I'd never been permitted to contact anyone.

When I stepped tremulously across the border into Brownsville, Texas, back into a country where The Constitution is usually respected, I nearly cried. You see, it took losing my rights for a while for me to finally appreciate them.

I recount this harrowing adventure every year in class. I am uncommonly grateful to be an American.

Don't get me wrong. I still often seethe with rage at our foreign policy and the public's ignorance and apathy regarding it. Now I merely employ a more patient, but ultimately more powerful, strategy to change them: education. I strive to make all my students proud of, and wary of, their government.

Dirty Diapers

Kudos to Maryland! In 1991, it became the first state to require public service for high school graduation. I wish Ohio had done the same when I was in high school. I had to wait until I was twenty-five to complete that part of my education.

I never would have volunteered on my own. There were so many other, apparently more enticing things to do with my summer vacation. Fortunately, a teacher-friend of mine twisted my arm so hard that, bewildered, I soon found myself among twelve other reluctant volunteers in the slums of Tijuana. We cursed our friends and our fate, but then got to work.

We helped out at an orphanage in a hillside barrio. One orphan, a small boy of about seven named Pablo, greeted me every day with a fierce bear hug. He was so starved for affection he wouldn't let go. He didn't want to share me with the rest of the kids. When I finally managed to pry him off, he'd alternately scream in anger or cry in anguish. After a few minutes, he'd sullenly join in the games. He never seemed to really enjoy them, though. Pablo so desperately wanted someone to pay attention to him, to love him and him alone.

Isabel was no different. Only a year old, she sat stoically in her high chair each lunchtime as I fed her and ten other infants in assembly-line fashion. I'd go down the line, Gerbers in hand, doling out spoonfuls of green glop. "Yum! Yum!" I lied.

Isabel became my favorite. Perhaps it was the astounding mess she could make in her diaper. None of the other volunteers wanted to change her, and, well, I was a sucker for her puppy-dog eyes. "Honestly, Isabel," I'd scold, "where did you get it all?"

Afterwards I paced the nursery with Isabel's head lying gently on my shoulder. I sang and rocked and tried everything I could to put her to sleep. But as soon as I placed her down, she'd turn her dark, despairing eyes on me and wail, her arms stretching out through the bars of her crib. Nonetheless, I had to go, even though I knew no one would pick her up again until dinner. Isabel, like Pablo, broke my heart.

As the month all too quickly drew to a close, I began to wonder if I was really helping any of the orphans. I'd made them depend on me. Then, like everyone else they'd ever known, I'd soon abandon them and return home, leaving them more utterly alone than ever. Perhaps it would have been better if I had never come.

Now, many years later, I realize my short volunteer service was not really supposed to help Pablo or Isabel, but to educate me to radically change my view of the world, and of myself. It did. Ever since, I have never once forgotten my own good fortune, or my responsibility to share it with others.

Students cannot learn that lesson in a classroom. That's why Maryland requires them to venture out into a complex, needy world to do so. I'm sure, like me, many will have to be dragged, kicking and screaming. Yet, although they may travel no farther than the nearest soup kitchen, most will return profoundly changed.

I hope, someday soon, most other states will follow Maryland's lead.

Mr. Murphy

IT'S STRANGE THAT OF ALL THE IMAGES I CHERISH OF MR. MURPHY, the one that remains the most vivid is of his palsied arm. I remember the evening was dreary, probably after a late rehearsal, and I had just helped Mr. Murphy into his car so his son could drive him home. Mr. Murphy's face was uncharacteristically fatigued, and his right arm hung lifelessly at his side. I had to lift it myself and place it nonchalantly on his lap before slamming the door.

As his car sped away, I felt my first pang of worry, the startling realization that The Great Mr. Murphy—icon, legend, god—was in fact oh so terribly mortal. He died two months later.

I could never pity Mr. Murphy, despite all his ailments. He made sure of that the first week of Freshman Speech class. He explained matter-of-factly how Polio had struck him as a young man, leaving him captive in his wheelchair, harnessed to a respirator. A few days later, in the middle of one of his lectures, he abruptly disconnected the respirator tube, stood shakily up, and limped to the podium. When he saw our eyes grow wide in astonishment, he feigned surprise. "Oh, didn't you know I could walk?" Then he grinned. The joke was on us. No, no one could pity Mr. Murphy.

Everyone respected him, though. In addition to speech, he taught government, and managed all the school's fund-raising. But it was his genius as a drama director that made his fame.

Mr. Murphy could deftly manage a pompous choreographer, an emotional music director, an unsteady conductor, and a cast and crew of well over a hundred immature students. He instilled in us all a deep love of the theater. More important, he taught us discipline, synergy, and pride. A good amount of my high school education, and virtually all of my growing up, took place after school, on his stage.

It wasn't easy for him, of course. Boy, could he lose his temper! All too often he'd defy his respirator and bellow out a "Shuuuuut uuuuuuuup!" loud enough to silence even a hall full of unruly teenagers.

Nor was I an angel. "Ellison, you're a damn ham," Mr. Murphy would growl, trying to put me in my place. Once he called backstage during a scene change, shrieking over the headphones, "You lose character on stage again and I'll lower the curtain!" He would've, too. I idolized him, but feared him just as much.

My senior year he gave me the lead in the spring musical. Then he beckoned me to his wheelchair. "I know you'll do fine, Dave," he encouraged me. "But don't forget: No one is indispensable. Not you. Not even me. The show will go on without us, so we can't get full of ourselves."

I wonder if he already knew he'd soon fulfill his own prophecy.

I dedicated all my performances to Mr. Murphy—not just the ones that spring, but all my succeeding roles as an actor and a teacher. I still can't ham it up without thinking of him.

It's not just because he died. In spite of a terrible physical fate, he worked tirelessly, joyfully, always in the service of others. And in doing so he taught me so much more than speech, or government and drama. Mr. Murphy taught me how to live.

Empty-Handed

As I splashed my way around the corner of the school building, I came upon Miguel, shivering forlornly beneath the roof overhang. He was trying desperately to remain both dry and unnoticed. Recently arrived from his small pueblo in the Mexican mountains, it was only his second day at school; and he was lost, unable to find his next class.

"That's easily remedied!" I casually assured him. I put my arm around him, guided him to the office, and obtained a new copy of his schedule. Just a few moments later I had already delivered him to Mr. Baine's math class, and was congratulating myself for a good deed easily done. It all seemed so simple.

Mr. Baine set me straight during lunch. "Miguel has never attended school before," he complained. "He's thirteen years old, but is totally illiterate. He can only barely count his age, even in Spanish; and I'm supposed to teach him algebra in English!"

I had to admit that the task seemed daunting.

Nonetheless, we were usually quite proud of our school's program for immigrant students. Heralding from around the globe, and speaking more than twenty different languages, they spent half a day together in a "sheltered" language arts/history class. Their teacher spoke nothing but English, yet reinforced everything she said with colorful pictures, giant posters, and elaborate gestures. Thus, she could slowly but miraculously develop her diverse group of students' English proficiency, while still giving them at least a watered-down version of the regular curriculum.

For the rest of the day the immigrant students were mainstreamed: They attended regular classes, like Mr. Baine's math class. You see, we wanted them to keep up academically with the other kids. And, what was even more important, we hoped they'd mingle with and ultimately befriend them too. After all, they'd learn most of their English from their newfound, American-born friends.

For most immigrants, the program was very successful. For instance, one of the guards on my basketball team had come from Yugoslavia only two years before. And he was earning As and Bs in all his classes. (He had a mean jump shot, too!)

But, of course, he'd been a successful student back in his war-ravaged homeland. Math and basketball were nothing new to him.

Miguel, on the other hand, had never been a student at all. Everything—from books and numbers to simply raising his hand—was strange. He desperately needed to become literate first in Spanish. Once he learned to love his own literature, and to comprehend a mathematical equation, then we might successfully mainstream him. The rest would be merely a matter of translation.

Unfortunately, we had no special classes for Miguel. Indeed, given our limited funding, we struggled just to maintain our existing program for immigrants. All we could do was watch helplessly while he wandered from class to incomprehensible class. No one was surprised when he finally gave up. One day a few weeks later, Miguel simply disappeared. We never saw him again.

There had been no schools in Miguel's remote, Mexican highland home. Perhaps that was one reason why he had abandoned it. But, if it was an education he sought, we disappointed him terribly.

All the Kids Are Fine

I LIKED DON AS A PERSON, AT FIRST. I CAME TO DESPISE HIM AS AN educator.

Don taught in my classroom during my prep period, so we traded jokes and complaints for a few moments almost every day. I might almost have called him a friend.

The trouble was, I soon recognized that Don was a politician. He was eager to move "up," out of the classroom, into the ranks of the administrators. He consistently found excuses to visit the district office, hoping the superintendents would notice him. He was so ingratiating, so subservient. Of course, all that was time and energy he was not directing toward his students.

Don's efforts finally paid off. He became the district liaison officer for the Language Development Program. I begrudged his promotion. Perhaps I was merely jealous. But I hated to see yet another salary go to someone without a classroom assignment.

Still, I hoped Don would accomplish something significant from his new, elevated position. I had long been frustrated with the Language Development Program. I trusted that he would listen to the problems, and then communicate them to the superintendents. I imagined he would be a catalyst for change. I was wrong.

One day I saw Don in the teachers' lounge after school. I sat down and told him the story of Miguel, an unfortunate boy from the highlands of Mexico. The deficiencies of our

Language Development Program had succeeded only in driving him away from school.

Don was unimpressed. He insisted the district's policy of heterogeneous grouping—keeping all kids together, regardless of their level of proficiency—was best. I asked how a kid who could barely count, even in his own language, would ever be successful in a normal eighth-grade math class. Don explained that the math teachers merely needed special training. I reminded him that Miguel's teacher was the most experienced and highly respected math instructor in the district. If he couldn't succeed, who could?

We bantered back and forth like this for nearly twenty minutes. I was relentless in my criticism of the Language Development Program. Yet, the more I harangued, the more defensive and angry Don became.

In retrospect, I think I understand why. Don knew what the superintendents wanted to hear—that heterogeneous grouping was working, even with a fourteen-year-old immigrant who had never before attended school. He gave them the good (but false) news they desired, and so earned their praise. Heaven forbid he should allow the welfare of children to get in the way of his career.

Last I heard, Don had finally become a superintendent himself—fortunately in another district far from mine. I'm sure he'll be very happy there in his new job at the top. But, what of all the children he abandoned along the way? Perhaps, like his predecessors, he'll simply surround himself with sycophantic administrative assistants who will tell him what he wants to hear: that all the kids are doing fine.

The Little Drummer Boy

How do you say good-bye to your best friend? Not the normal good-bye, such as when two teens might head off to different colleges, wishing each other luck. No, Deonte's friend, Steven, was dying. There would be no college for him, nor even, perhaps, a tomorrow. This would be no ordinary good-bye.

Of course, Steven was no ordinary friend. Deonte had met him in the first grade, and remained in the same class with him for the next five years. They'd played baseball, football, and basketball together. In the school band, Steven played the trumpet, Deonte the drums. The two looked forward to the day when they'd finally don their uniforms, and go on tour with the varsity band.

Over the years, Deonte learned to depend on Steven. As bright as Deonte was, he tried the patience of many a principal, teacher, and coach, including me. He relied on Steven's calming presence, his steady example, to keep him on the straight and narrow.

Then the fickle hand of fate struck Steven with leukemia.

Everyone clung to hope. There was chemotherapy, and maybe even a bone-marrow transplant. Steven would pull through. He just had to. After all, he was a straight-A student, winning all sorts of academic and service awards. Everybody liked him.

But leukemia, ever merciless, didn't take any of that into account. It continued its unrelenting ravage until, finally,

Steven left the hospital for the last time. There was nothing more the doctors could do. Steven came home to die.

It was only then that Deonte accepted the awful fact that he'd have to say good-bye to Steven, forever. But how?

That evening, the entire band assembled in front of Steven's house. Many teachers, students, and neighbors gathered as well, hugging and consoling each other, all struggling to maintain a strained smile for Steven.

He finally emerged, doped with morphine, confined to a wheelchair, sucking air through an oxygen mask. Nonetheless, his indomitable spirit had prevailed over his weakened body: He sported a broad smile, and the glittering band uniform he had always longed to wear. No wonder Deonte liked him so much!

How could Deonte play, tucked away in the back of the band with the rest of the drums? It just didn't seem enough. He needed Steven to see him, to hear him. So, quietly, he moved to the front, and stationed himself right next to Steven. The director, D.C., gave him a nod, and lifted his baton. Then the concert began.

And Deonte played for him, ba-rum-pa-pa-pum. The brass and winds kept time, ba-rum-pa-pa-pum. He played his drum for him, ba-rum-pa-pa-pum. He played his best for him, ba-rum-pa-pa-pum, rum-pa-pa-pum, rum-pa-pa-pum. He and his drum.

It was an incredibly beautiful, simple, profound gesture— one befitting the birth of a King, and the death of Deonte's best friend.

God Bless Them, Every One

I WAS HAUNTED BY THREE SPIRITS.

I sat eating a bag-lunch in San Francisco's Union Square, marveling at the tallest Christmas tree I'd ever seen, while keeping a wary eye on my eighth graders as they gleefully romped from bench to bush to tree. Clearly our field trip to a production of Dickens' *A Christmas Carol* was a scintillating adventure for them, and for me. You see, I rarely had such leisure to appreciate my students for the remarkable, unfathomable individuals they are.

Most of the kids gathered in small groups, as is their wont, betraying their various personalities and allegiances. The sight of Adam standing alone, however, conjured up the unbidden ghost of some terrible Christmas past, which had left him scarred both physically and emotionally. Bright but unskilled, polite but aloof, Adam worried me. So far I'd failed to help him, comprehend him, or even converse with him. So had everyone else.

Across the square, as unobtrusive as possible, sat Sylvia and Richard, together. Birds of a feather, I mused.

I'd called Sylvia's home just days before, only to discover that mom lived elsewhere, dad was on the road, and grandma was asleep. Apparently Sylvia would have to raise herself. We spoke for a bit about how she must learn to be more responsible, much more mature. She'd seemed flattered by our impromptu man-to-woman chat. But, would she finally do her work? Would she be able to resist the advances of the older high school boys next year, who'd mark her easy prey?

Richard, meanwhile, faced an awful choice himself. I'd asked him once, "How many of your friends in the gang earned a college degree? How many have so much as a high school diploma? Beware, Richard. You will become who your friends are. You're going to have to choose, the gang or an education."

Such simplistic advice! I'd urged him to "just say no" to virtually everything, everyone he'd ever known. What kind of viable alternative could I provide?

There they sat, Sylvia and Richard, chatting innocently, oblivious to the dark specter of their future, fraught with peril.

A shout from one of my students startled me, dispelling my woeful reveries. I quickly glanced around the park where the other kids still frolicked with barely concealed wonder at all the exotic sights and discordant sounds of The City, resplendent in its holiday finery. Even a Scrooge like me couldn't help but laugh along with them.

Before we left, I spied Adam edging his way toward a group of boys who were pestering some pigeons, and he joined shyly in their mischief. Later I looked back over at Sylvia and Richard. They did make an awfully cute couple. And hadn't they come together for tutoring last week?

So, the Spirit of Christmas Present won out in the end. Yes, often the world's still cruel to children, just as it was in Dickens' day. But there's still hope for them as well, and sometimes even joy.

Indeed, I finally led my students Pied-Piper-like along San Francisco's bustling sidewalks to the theater, where Dickens had his magical way with them. And, along with Tiny Tim, I prayed God would bless them, every one.

Fleeing Fleeting Time

I'M DEPRESSED. NORMALLY MY JOB INSULATES ME FROM THE passage of time. My students are perennially thirteen or fourteen years old. Their names and faces change every September, but they remain young and innocent; and so, by association, do I. Or, at least that's how I like to deceive myself.

It's becoming harder to do so lately. Last week, for example, I heard from a long-lost teacher-friend of mine from Texas. After we had reminisced for a while, he remarked that he had bumped into Rosa, one of my former sixth-grade students, who had asked about me. I was flattered. One of my kids actually remembered me! I decided to write Rosa right after I hung up the phone.

Well, I got half way through the letter before I realized I was writing it as if I were still addressing a twelve-year-old. I had imagined that Rosa hadn't changed in all the intervening years. But she had to be at least twenty! "Why, she's a young woman already," I said to myself in disbelief, and horror. "What does that make me?"

I had a hard time finishing the letter.

I usually manage to avoid such rude awakenings. I've wandered from school to school, from state to state. I've never lingered long enough to witness my students grow up. No, I have preserved them safe in my memory, forever little kids.

Now that I've worked at Barnard-White for many years, though (if I don't watch myself, I just might sink some roots!), it's becoming nearly impossible to ignore the fleeting years. My

God, the students I first taught here must be . . . twenty-eight years old! How dare they?

One of them had the impertinence to visit me the other day. I was helping time the runners at a track meet after school when I heard a strange, deep voice accost me: "Hello there, Mr. Ellison!"

I turned around and found myself staring at somebody's chest. Then I looked up into a face I only vaguely recognized.

"Don't you remember me, Mr. Ellison? It's me, Alex!"

Alex? Not the puny kid with the munchkin voice. Impossible! "Why, of course I remember you, Alex! How have you been?"

And so began a lengthy, torturous conversation in which my little Alex—now gargantuan—recounted all his adventures: College, girlfriends, a trip abroad, a new job. He was handsome, confident, mature, well-rounded. A gloriously bright future awaited him, and he was eager to discover it.

And then Alex did something really cruel: "So, you still teaching the same thing at Barnard, Mr. Ellison?"

I could have killed him. Suddenly my life seemed so mundane, such a rut. I hobbled home to stare despairingly at myself in the mirror, count the burgeoning wrinkles around my eyes, caress the defiant strands atop my head, and sigh. Wasn't it just yesterday that I, too, was young and adventurous? How did Alex grow so tall, and I so old?

My colleagues tell me to relax: "Wait until you find yourself teaching Alex's children, Dave."

Never! I wonder if there are any teaching jobs in Alaska.

Pendulums

IN 1789, THE FRENCH DREAMED OF CREATING UTOPIA. AFTER storming the Bastille and eventually beheading King Louis XVI, they declared a republic of "liberty, equality, and fraternity."

Viva la naïveté! You see, in this imperfect, messy world of ours, liberty with equality is unattainable. Pure equality, for example, can be achieved only at the expense of personal freedoms, as the communists demonstrated. Similarly, unbridled liberty invariably leads to a terribly unequal distribution of wealth, as we capitalists have discovered. In other words, in politics and economics, we can't both have our cake and eat it too.

The same proves true for most educational issues. The controversy surrounding basic skills and higher-ordered thinking (phonics versus whole language) provides an apt example. Both extremes have led us to disaster. Hopefully we've learned from our mistakes, and will now pursue a blended approach.

There are innumerable instances of such difficult dilemmas. Some people demand that their neighborhoods control their local schools. The problem is that this engenders outrageous disparities between rich and poor schools—an injustice many state supreme courts have declared unconstitutional. California's did in 1976. Now every school in California has at least a basic minimum of funding. Unfortunately, every school is burdened with a massive state bureaucracy as well. Either way we lose.

How about tracking or heterogeneous grouping? When we tried sorting kids according to ability—into reading groups like the bluebirds, the redbirds, and the crows—we ended up inadvertently dividing youngsters according to their socioeconomic backgrounds. Poor students, too often kids of color, found themselves placed with the crows, a lower track from which they never escaped.

Oh, we're wiser now, and keep most kids together. Nonetheless, with one child in a class reading on a fourth-grade level, and another who's ready for high school texts, it's often an overwhelming challenge indeed to meet individual needs.

Then there's "site-based management," a current educational buzzword, which posits that each school should be left alone to make its own decisions. The price?—there's always one hidden somewhere, you know! Encouraging every school to march to the beat of a different drummer is a woefully inefficient use of resources. In addition, schools invariably become so different that parents fight to get their kids into the one perceived to be the best—and perception is not always reality.

My district, on the other hand, has made equity its watchword, regimenting it with strict, top-down centrally controlled cadences. As a result, the district is financially sound, but—here comes the price—it has often stifled the creativity and initiative at its various schools.

So, what's the answer? Should I have my kids study individually or in teams? Should I plan active projects or make a real attempt at completing the curriculum? Teach western civilization or embrace multiculturalism? Foster self-esteem or enforce strict discipline? Aaagh!

Education abounds with such dilemmas, tough choices between apparently desirable but mutually exclusive goals. The best we can do is finally stop the pendulums from swinging erratically from one extreme to another, strive for some uneasy balance, and then reconcile ourselves to feeling dissatisfied still.

Perhaps, though, once we accept that there can be no utopia, we'll stop shouting at each other, begin to compromise, and maybe even achieve that last of French ideals, *fraternity*.

Sorry

"WHAT THE HELL'S THE MATTER WITH YOU, CINDY? DON'T YOU give a damn about anyone except yourself?"

Those angry words of mine would haunt me for the rest of the year, and color forever my relationship with one of my students, Cindy. I blurted them one day when my students were working on a project in teams. Cindy—clearly bright but ever caustic—had publicly humiliated a less-gifted, shy boy on her team, and I'd called her back to my desk for a thorough dressing down.

I was furious. Soon, Cindy was too. And it was she who ultimately put me in my place. Before the day ended she'd already complained to the principal about my outrageous profanity. You see, in her version, she embellished a bit, substituting some other, more colorful four-letter words in place of *hell* and *damn*.

To this day I bristle at the memory of the ensuing investigation, which involved the principal, two assistant principals, one parent, and three student witnesses. I was on the defensive, blushing, stammering, struggling to defend my reputation before my peers. Even though I finally proved I hadn't uttered the awful words Cindy claimed, I did have to apologize for the unwise ones I had used. Meanwhile, Cindy apologized for nothing.

Afterwards, noticing my lingering rage, the principal asked pointedly, "Dave, can you still teach Cindy? Perhaps I should move her to another class."

"No," I sighed after a few, pensive moments, "I lost my temper, and Cindy cunningly seized the opportunity to turn the tables. I deserved it. Besides, I have to grudgingly admire her. She really used her head. Now I'd like to teach her to use her heart as well. I'll be fine."

I wasn't, though. Oh, I kept my cool for the rest of the year, even in the face of Cindy's persistent, ugly defiance. I even complimented her insights often in class.

But I kept my distance as well. While I was frivolously silly with other kids, I remained cautious, cold, professional in my interactions with Cindy. I told myself this was only prudent. In retrospect, however, I believe it was my form of subtle vengeance. I withheld from Cindy the warmth I lavished on others, and so hoped to exact a heavy price for having embarrassed me. I succeeded. Cindy never smiled for the rest of the year.

Nonetheless, on the last day of school, Cindy once again turned the tables. She waited after class, awkwardly thrust a small box into my hands, and then vanished out the door. Inside the box was a beautiful tie.

I stared at it a long while. Was it a belated apology? Was it a thank-you for at least treating her with respect? Was it a futile attempt to buy back my affection? It didn't really matter, I suppose, because it was too late. The year was over. Cindy was gone.

I won't forget Cindy, or our strained year together. I stubbornly waited for a young lady to ask my forgiveness. In the end, it was I who was sorry.

Bringing Out Our Best

I KNOW JOSÉ WILL NEVER BE ABLE TO READ THIS LETTER. FATE, ever capricious, gave him an extra chromosome. He has Downs Syndrome, and is severely mentally retarded. He's fourteen, and yet functions at a four-year-old's level. No, José will never read this, nor do a multitude of other basic things the rest of us take for granted.

José isn't alone, of course. There are twenty-nine other severely handicapped kids who come to Barnard-White on a special bus every day.

They're all well taken care of. Three teachers and six aides greet them with enormous smiles and infinite patience each morning. In addition, a school psychologist, a speech specialist, and an adaptive physical education teacher stop by periodically. They're all part of an extremely expensive program—one that most private or charter schools wouldn't even consider—dedicated to the proposition that all kids deserve an education. Everybody, no matter what, ought to have an opportunity to go as far as he or she can.

Unfortunately, it's unlikely José will ever get very far. As I watched him in the classroom laboring with his pencil, I realized success in a classroom of severely handicapped kids must be measured in small accomplishments.

For example, after four years at Barnard-White, José can write his first name—with jagged, but legible letters. He can copy his last name and address, and even recognize every numeral up to nine. He's learned to go to the bathroom by himself, feed himself, and keep himself neat and clean. Best of all, he can now talk using simple words and short phrases.

Perhaps José's greatest achievement has been a newfound self-confidence. He no longer sits silently at his desk, keeping his head down in shame, fear, or frustration. Now he slaps people five, and says, "Hey Dude!" He plays silly practical jokes on the psychologist. And he blows kisses to the pretty women who visit class.

Of course, no one in his eyes will ever replace his teacher, Ms. Valdez. José regularly steals flowers from his front yard and brings them sheepishly to her, hiding them behind his back. "He's a real charmer," she confided to me. "Yes, he's come a long way."

His father put it best: "José isn't as frustrated as he once was. He's a lot happier, and so am I." There is much to celebrate.

In a few weeks José will don a blue gown and graduate with all the other eighth graders at school. We haven't hidden him away from them, secluding him in a special school like we used to do. No, they've watched José learn and grow—albeit a lot more slowly—right along with themselves. In fact, many of them have spent innumerable hours volunteering in his classroom.

It's funny: Some of those student-tutors were discipline problems in their regular classes. But whenever they had the chance to help José, they became strangely quiet, suddenly caring, and astonishingly mature. Somehow, José brought out the best in them.

Perhaps that is why educating José was very important, even though we'll never enable him to read this. In struggling for minor miracles, we affirm the dignity and worth of all kids—no matter what their ability or disability.

Yes, José is really special. He brings out the best in us all.

Last Hurrah

"I WASN'T GOING TO GO ON THE EARLY-BIRD HIKE," JENNY guilelessly revealed our first morning at Point Reyes. "But then I heard you were leading it, so here I am!"

I stopped and stared at her, stunned.

"What's wrong?" she asked, staring back with her big, hazel eyes.

"I don't think we're in Kansas anymore, Toto," I responded cryptically.

"What?"

"Oh, nothing. I'm just glad you came, Jenny. Let's get a move on. We don't want to be late for breakfast!" Together we trudged down the trail, many other fifth graders following eagerly, in single file behind us.

It would have been difficult for me to explain my confusion that morning. You see, I usually spend my days with eighth graders. They express affection only with some sort of insult. It's when they toss off some snide remark about my hairline or my clothes that I know they like me. So Jenny's simple candor caught me off guard. It was the first of many similar, pleasant surprises during the fifth-graders' outdoor education trip.

After breakfast, for example, the camp director announced it was time to clean the cabins. The kids from the best cabin would be first in the lunch line. Jenny and her classmates squealed in delight, and dashed off to fight over the brooms. I shook my head in disbelief.

"If these were my eighth graders," I told the director, "we'd have to threaten them with death or worse to get even a few to grudgingly pick up a broom."

"Take a good look, Dave," he responded. "These kids are on the threshold of adolescence. In a little while hormones will poison them too."

He was right. Jenny couldn't imagine the transformation that awaited her and her friends. The boys would learn to swagger and to hide behind a macho facade. The girls—perhaps even Jenny—would become moody and put on their own masks of lipstick and hair spray. It's all a part of the gauntlet that is puberty.

But, for the moment, Jenny was still an innocent, little girl. That was never more clear than later that afternoon, when she ran up to tattle on a friend.

"Ricky called me a virgin!" she complained. Then, after a pause, "What's a virgin?"

I stifled a smile, and explained: "A virgin is a wonderful person who decides to save herself for the one she loves. It is something to be proud of. In fact, the first settlers in America named their colony after their virgin queen, Elizabeth. They called the colony 'Virginia.' Ricky must like you, Jenny."

"That jerk? I hate him!" And she ran off to spend the rest of the afternoon telling him so.

That night at the campfire, Jenny and her friends were still naive enough to be frightened by the camp director's traditional ghost story. And they were still unselfconscious enough to sing lustily together. Yet, those joyful songs were, perhaps, the last hurrah of their childhood.

A Box of Raisins

IN THE END, THE TRIP WAS A SUCCESS FOR FRANK, THANKS TO ONE small box of raisins.

I had been so busy during the first day at Point Reyes—helping the fifth graders find their cabins, and planning hikes—that I hadn't had an opportunity to speak with Frank. But I was awfully glad he'd accompanied his son, Shane, on the Outdoor Education Trip. He had made himself invaluable in the kitchen, assuming the responsibilities of both head-cook and chief-dishwasher. He seemed a man obsessed with helping out.

I learned the next day, however, that he had merely been assuaging his disappointment, and his guilt.

Frank and I stood on the beach together, chuckling at the antics of the kids as they dodged the waves in Sir Francis Drake Bay. How could they endure that cold water?

"It's funny," Frank commented. "I grew up on the ocean. Now I seldom find myself even at a beach like this." He went on to tell of his own childhood, spent on his father's fishing boat. I asked if such a youth was as wholesome as I imagined.

"No," he answered. "My father was cruel." After an uncomfortable moment of silence, he added, "I've struggled to avoid the same mistakes with Shane. I'm afraid I've failed." He sighed heavily, turned away, and walked alone down the beach, his hands in his pockets, his pants flapping violently in the wind.

Frank had recently divorced, and didn't see Shane so much anymore. But now he had taken three days off from work to come on this trip. He'd hoped to spend some "quality time" with him, and perhaps even begin to make amends.

Shane, however, would have none of it. In fact, so far he had shunned Frank completely. He had refused to accompany him in the car on the way up, choosing instead to ride with his friends on the bus. Nor would he sit next to Frank at mealtimes, or hike anywhere near him on the trails. He didn't even acknowledge his dad with so much as a "Good morning." Kids can be cruel too.

As I watched Shane play on the sand, ignoring his dad as usual, I understood why Frank had been immersing himself so intently in kitchen duties.

Frank's patience finally wore Shane down, though. A half hour later, Shane had tired of the Pacific. Shivering, his teeth chattering, he approached the fire we had built on the beach. Frank sat on a log, off by himself.

Shane first asked the camp director for his snack ration, a box of raisins. Then he hesitated, looking first at the fire, then at his dad. He chose dad. He sat on Frank's lap, wet pants and all, and snuggled in the towel dad wrapped around him. Together they shared the box of raisins.

The next morning, as we were loading the bus to return to Union City, we were one student short.

"It's Shane," one of the kids explained. "He went home with his dad."

It was a very good trip, indeed.

A Damn Shame

MARCH HAS COME AND GONE, BUT THE FIFTH GRADERS HAVEN'T made their yearly pilgrimage to Point Reyes. Like so many other student programs, the Outdoor Education Trip has slipped quietly into oblivion. And I am sad.

The project began seven years ago, the brainchild of an uncommonly inspired group of fifth-grade teachers. They were young, energetic, idealistic, and terrified. And so they learned to depend on each other. They ate together, planned together, played together, and soon made the fifth grade one of the strongest, most cohesive departments at Barnard-White.

Nonetheless, their job still wasn't easy. I can imagine how frustrating it was to teach science to youngsters who couldn't tell the difference between a bay and an oak tree, a sea otter or a sea lion. Many had never even seen the Pacific. What did they care about photosynthesis, food chains, or ecology?

Eventually, a few teachers went crazy: "Hey, we need to get our students out into nature so that they can see for themselves what they're studying. Let's take them camping!" Hundreds of hours of searching, meeting, phone calling, and fund-raising later, they did.

The first March, two fifth-grade classes spent three days at Battery Alexander on the Marin Headlands. They slept in the dreary, damp, cavernous bunkers. They ate frosted flakes, peanut butter sandwiches, and hot dogs. The teachers returned with dark circles under their eyes. But the kids brought back bright smiles and many tales of adventure. (Their story of the death march through the jungle of poison oak was exaggerated, I'm sure.) Best of all, they had learned the names and life cycles of many of the little critters they'd seen scurrying in the forest and along the beach.

Everything snowballed from there. Two years later, nearly every fifth grader traveled to the project's new home at Point Reyes. Filling in for one teacher, I led an early-bird morning hike and conducted the afternoon tree-identification class. I made the mistake of remarking that Bay leaves were used to season soups and sauces. Well, every single kid insisted on contributing a leaf to the evening's dinner. The ensuing spaghetti was outrageously pungent—the best the kids had ever tasted.

Like the kids, I will always remember dodging the afternoon waves at Sir Francis Drake Bay, greeting the deer on their evening trek through the meadow, and watching the sparks from the late-night campfire rise to take their place among the constellations. There was something mystical about the fifth-grade Outdoor Education Trip.

But all things must pass. The Point Reyes board of directors began to discourage poorer schools, which couldn't afford to hire the park's naturalists or stay for a full week. Back at Barnard, money was scarcer than ever. Student fund-raisers were needed for other programs. Meanwhile, many of the young fifth-grade teachers married, settled down, and had kids of their own. They could no longer go so far above and beyond the call of duty.

This March, the fifth graders went nowhere. The Golden Age of the fifth grade is over.

It was inevitable, I suppose. But it was also a damn shame.

Blah, Blah, Blah

I READ A FAR SIDE CARTOON ONCE THAT WENT SOMETHING LIKE this: A man stood pointing his finger at a dog. The caption beneath read, "Now listen, Ginger, I want you to stop burying your bones in the garden. . . .' " The next frame was identical except for the caption, "What dogs hear: 'Blah, blah, Ginger, blah, blah, blah, blah. . . .' "

Joni intercepted the note during her fourth-period science class. She was accustomed to such illicit messages, as she already had five years' experience teaching junior high school students. (There will be a special place for her in heaven.)

Joni had come to her profession late in life, after overcoming myriad obstacles including one sexist high school guidance counselor long ago. She still recalled with righteous rage his advice: that in order to ever become a science teacher, she'd have to take physics; and, well, that would really be much too hard for her. Only boys took that course. She ought to consider something else.

Joni had foolishly acquiesced, set her dreams aside, only to rekindle them many years later. She ended up earning an A in physics, perhaps more out of spite than anything else.

Now she was determined to prove to all her students, especially the girls, that they could accomplish anything, be anything. She was living proof.

And there she stood, staring down at the impertinent note, a dialogue between two of her young, female students. Off-task again. It was maddening! She read:

"Isn't Ms. G. great?" the first girl had written.

"Yeah, I really admire her," the second had replied.

Joni took a long, triumphant breath. She'd succeeded! She'd become the powerful role model she'd so aspired to be! All those years of anguished struggle and persistence had paid off. Now, perhaps, these young girls might study physics one day, maybe even become scientists!

Unfortunately, Joni continued reading to the end of the note: "Yep. G.s cool. I wish my hair looked like hers. I wonder where she gets her nails done. . . ."

Michael was a new teacher, still clinging to the naive idealism that brings many such bright college graduates into a classroom. He taught language arts and history, hoping to impart not only a love of the English language and literature, but also an appreciation for the Earth's continents and cultures.

One boy, however, remained apathetic. He'd done no homework, passed no exams.

So, one morning after Michael had gotten the class started on a silent-reading activity, he crouched next to the boy, and cajoled him. "I know you can do it," he whispered in conclusion.

Just before he stood to leave, though, Michael remembered from his teacher education classes how he ought to get the student to talk at least a bit, make the encounter a conversation instead of just a scolding. "Do you have anything you'd like to say or ask?" he inquired hopefully.

The boy rolled his eyes at the ceiling, and then responded, "Do you like wearing corduroy pants?"

Michael blinked a few times, took a deep breath, and then answered tersely, "Get to work."

What children hear: "Blah, blah, blah, blah. . . ."

Wrestling Stereotypes

ANISSA CROUCHED LOW, CIRCLING HER OPPONENT, HER NARROWED eyes revealing both fear and determination. A fifth grader, she stood all of four foot three, and weighed sixty-four pounds. The height, weight, or age of her adversary mattered little, since he was a boy. Everyone believed he must win.

Suddenly the boy had Anissa in a fierce hold, lifted her high, and then threw her viciously back to the ground. There was no chivalry in school wrestling, particularly during a finals match.

Anissa's father gasped on the sidelines. Wouldn't someone step in and stop the contest, make sure his daughter was all right?

Dad had attended all Anissa's matches, but this was the first time he'd actually seen Anissa wrestle. Every one of her previous opponents had refused to fight. It was somewhat understandable because, for boys, it seemed to be a lose–lose situation: Beat a girl and everyone would treat the victory with scorn; lose and, well, the humiliation would be unendurable. So they had chosen to forfeit.

This, however, was the championship. This boy had to fight. And it was clear from his ruthless tactics that, no matter what it took, he intended to win.

As dad watched his daughter pick herself up, he swallowed hard. Perhaps it was a blessing he had forgotten the camcorder. But, he noted with surprise, there was something new in his daughter's eyes—anger.

The score was ten to ten, with time running out. Relentless, desperate, the boy attacked again, this time going for Anissa's legs. Anissa deftly dodged him, though, and tripped him as he went by. Then she was on him, trapping him in a half nelson the coach had taught her. Thus, Anissa garnered two points for a takedown, just as time expired. She had won. She'd become the first girl from Barnard-White Middle School to win a finals match.

"I told Anissa I didn't think it was a good idea for her to wrestle," her mom mused afterwards. "But then she asked me, 'Is it because I'm a girl?' What could I say? I had always taught her she could do anything."

Indeed, that was the underlying message of Women's History Month in March. We educators passed on the inspiring stories of Susan B. Anthony, Sojourner Truth, Elizabeth Blackwell . . . women who courageously pushed the limit of their role in society. Like Anissa's mom, we held them up as models, assuring girls that they, too, could do anything, be anything.

But, a wrestler? Or a combat soldier? A priest? President? Our discomfort reveals that the crusade for women's rights and equality is far from over.

As long as there are singular youngsters like Anissa and the four other girls on the Barnard wrestling team, however, who dare to take us adults at our word, the struggle will continue. "We wanted to do something that girls don't usually do," Anissa explained.

Susan B. Anthony would be proud. And so should we.

Hemorrhoids

CARLOS COULD MAKE IT, DESPITE HIMSELF. OF COURSE, HE'D HAVE every excuse if he failed. He'd never known a father, and his mother had been brutally murdered in a drug deal down by the tracks. Now he lived with his grandparents who, although they loved him, didn't quite know what to do with him. As he grew older, they became more afraid. And so did he. Only thirteen, and yet, unwittingly, he faced difficult, dangerous choices.

I remember Halloween when Carlos came to school dressed as a gang member. With dark glasses, a red bandanna (which I confiscated), and a penciled-in mustache, he played the role so well he startled me. I guessed—or, perhaps, only hoped—that his donning the costume was merely a queer, desperate attempt to distance himself from the role, to call it a masquerade, something fake he could discard with ease at any time.

Carlos wanted to escape the barrio. I often told him a good education was his way out, and I think he half believed me. Every now and again he'd turn in some impressive work just to reassure himself—and me?—that he really could do it. Yet, more often he shied away from academic success, fleeing that insidious label, "school boy," which would mean banishment from his friends. How could I—an adult, a *güero*—speak more convincingly than they?

I thought for a time that Carlos hated me. He peppered my lessons with arrogant defiance, playing Devil's Advocate with many ideas I expressed, nearly every instruction I gave. One afternoon, though, I witnessed him do the same with another teacher. When she took his bait and engaged him in an angry debate, I noticed his disappointment.

Thus, Carlos taught me I would never win an argument with him, or any adolescent for that matter. And, in his incessant attempts to tear me and other adults down, he finally revealed his dogged search for someone to respect. He'd never admit it, not even to himself, but perhaps he was hoping one of us would one day win.

That's why I began to counter so many of his "What for?s" with a terse, "Because I'm mean and nasty. Now get to work!" I left him no reply. He was shocked at first. Later he only mumbled beneath his breath. Nonetheless, class by class, he challenged less, seemed to listen more. And when, after one brief, particularly harsh rebuke I leaned down and whispered, "It's my hemorrhoids, Carlos. That's why I'm so bad," he actually smirked. What's more important, he did get to work.

Yes, I had high hopes for Carlos. Maybe he did for me too.

Chewing Gum, Lipstick, and a B

ROSA SUCCEEDED, IN SPITE OF ME.

I remember the very first thing I said to her, just after she entered my classroom in September. "Spit that gum out right now!"

I recognized the kind of girl she was. She wore the requisite black pants and red shirt of the Decoto gang. The uniform included dark lipstick surrounded by black liner, rouge, over-done-up hair, and, of course, chewing gum. Unfortunately, the only thing in my power to control was the gum.

As Rosa slid into her seat with a scowl, I shook my head and sighed in resignation. I'd seen so many girls like her before. I knew what to expect: She'd arrive late to class nearly every day. If she wasn't inattentive and apathetic, she'd be insolent and disruptive. She'd rarely do her homework; and even on those few occasions when she did, she'd merely reveal how poor her skills were.

I didn't think through that pessimistic scenario consciously. In fact, I wasn't really aware of how terribly I had prejudged Rosa until I computed grades a few weeks later. There, next to her name was a B.

"Impossible," I muttered to myself. I quickly scanned back through my records looking for the error in my calculations. But there was none. The B was correct. Rosa was a good student after all.

Boy, was I surprised! And that surprise shocked, embarrassed, and frightened me.

I had studied devastating research in graduate school regarding such teacher expectations. One group of teachers had been informed that, as a part of an experiment, they would instruct a special class of gifted children. The other teachers were told the opposite—that they would receive the troubled, low-skilled students. What both groups of teachers didn't know was that all the classes were nearly identical, random selections of kids.

At the end of the semester, the results told an awful story. The teachers of the *smart* classes remarked how much they'd enjoyed themselves, and how well their students had done. And, in fact, testing revealed that the kids really had learned a lot.

Meanwhile, both the teachers and the students in the other classes had had a miserable time, and tests confirmed the kids had learned very little.

Such is the incredible power of teacher expectations. Students will usually behave and perform exactly the way their teachers expect them to.

I had expected the worst out of Rosa. She had succeeded anyway. Perhaps her parents or a previous, more-enlightened teacher had convinced her to believe in herself, no matter what a prejudiced man like me might say or do.

But what of other kids who hadn't been so blessed? How many of them had I unconsciously convinced they could never do well? How many of all the Ds and Fs some of my students earned were more a reflection of my dismal expectations than of the students' actual talents?

I stared at Rosa's B a long time, chagrinned.

The next day I greeted Rosa at the door with an uncharacteristic smile. And she smiled back. For the first time, I noticed how beautiful she was—not like a gang member at all.

007

I'VE PRIDED MYSELF ON MY ABILITY TO SPOT GUM CHEWERS AT fifty paces. And when I do, I usually subject them to my infamous, scathing lecture: "Now, you knew when you put that gum in your mouth that you were breaking the rules. What's the matter with you?"

I don't fool myself, of course. I know that, once around the corner, the miscreants will stick another wad of gum in their mouths. Kids these days!

But yesterday when I nabbed Francie chomping on some Double Bubble trouble, I couldn't even begin my customary tirade. You see, I'd have been a hypocrite.

Over the weekend I had gone to an Oakland A's game with a bunch of other teachers, including my principal. On my way to meet them at the stadium, I'd stopped by a convenience store to pick up three cold sodas. It wasn't until I came to the Coliseum gate that I'd remembered cans were forbidden in the stadium.

"Dang!" I thought to myself. "I can't let these sodas go to waste!" I pondered the problem for a while, and then hit on a devious plan: I'd smuggle them in.

I went around the corner and, as inconspicuously as possible, hid the sodas beneath my jacket, holding them in the small of my back with my loosened belt. I knew the guards would check my pack; but they wouldn't frisk me. Ingenious!

As I approached the gate, I imagined I was a secret agent, attempting to smuggle a microdot through Checkpoint Charlie.

I tried to appear nonchalant, and calmly handed the guard my pack. A moment later he carelessly waved me on through.

There was a moment of terror, just after I passed the gate. One of the cans slipped free and began to slide down into my pants. Gasp! How would I explain myself if an illicit can plopped out from my pants' leg? Fortunately, I hobbled to my seat before anyone noticed what was going on.

"Ah, I fooled them all!" I thought with glee. I had yet again saved the Free World! Or, at least I'd have my three cans of soda.

With a mischievous grin, I opened the first can. It's funny how the fact that it was contraband made it taste even better.

"Hey you!" It was one of the ushers! "Yeah, you with the soda can. Come on, get your things together. You're out of here!" My principal rolled her eyes in embarrassment.

The usher marched me to the nearest trashcan and, to the amusement of all around, made me pour out all three cans, one by one. "Now, you knew when you brought them in that you were breaking the rules! What's the matter with you?"

I cowered in shame, and profusely pleaded for mercy, the fate of the Free World forgotten.

Well, the usher relented. (Bless his soul!)

Chastened, I slunk back to my seat—to be greeted by the wild applause of my colleagues, and the stern, shaking head of my principal.

That's why I spared Francie my usual lecture. It was my turn to show a little mercy. I merely asked her to spit the gum out.

And, as she trotted off to the trashcan, I smiled and reminisced that it really wasn't so long ago that I myself was a disobedient teenager. Like, last weekend for instance.

Teachers these days!

Grandma

"I'M ONE YEAR YOUNGER THAN GOD," GRANDMA TELLS THE KIDS whenever they ask her age. Actually, she's seventy-eight. And her real name is Helen, although few call her that anymore. To students and teachers alike, she's our Grandma.

I remember when Grandma first appeared as hall monitor. My God, I thought. What idiot hired such a sweet old lady? Why, the students will eat her alive the first day! They'll give her a stroke or a heart attack!

The kids really tried. "They hoped to startle me," Grandma reminisced, "and to be honest, they succeeded. But I never let my shock show. I either ignored their vulgar language, or I laughed. Now they're embarrassed to say anything rude around me. They know I love them!"

They love her back. "She acts like one of us," one girl explained. "She knows how to play around. The other day I went to her to complain that a boy was teasing me. 'What's the matter sweetheart?' she asked. (I love when she calls me that!) When I told her, she said, 'Well, you probably deserved it! I'll tease you too!' She made me laugh, and I forgot I was mad!"

Grandma walks nearly five miles through the halls every day, conspicuous with her pink baseball cap, matching tennis shoes, and dark sunglasses. She urges the kids to hustle to class, opens restrooms in an "emergency," and alerts the office with her walkie-talkie when anything out of the ordinary happens.

But Grandma sees her job as much more than that. "Perhaps I give the children one thing, and that is wisdom. For example, I tell them 'Do it once, do it right, and you won't have to do it again. Otherwise, life will pass you by!'

"School has changed so much since I was a child," she mused. "Of course, I've been around a while. I remember when coffee was five cents a cup, and shows were twenty-five cents. Now that's a long time ago! Back then, kids respected their teachers. And parents were more supportive. They weren't so 'sue' conscious."

I asked Grandma what she liked most about the job. "Oh, the hugs and the kisses from the little ones, and the respect from the older ones. But my best moment was during the academic awards assembly, when I performed with the rest of the staff. I was so nervous! But, as I stepped out onto the stage in my costume, the kids gave me a standing ovation. I'll always remember that."

Her worst day? "Never had one," she responded. "I do get awfully tired of opening doors, though. The other day, in fact, I had a terrible nightmare. I dreamt I had died and was before Saint Peter at the gates of heaven. He gave me an enormous ring of keys. 'Oh no!' I asked him. 'Will I need to unlock doors in heaven too?' When he nodded, I told him, 'Well, then, I'm not going!'"

Grandma, that suits us just fine.

Square Peg

I KNEW JACOB WAS UP TO SOMETHING WHEN HE CAME TO CLASS that day, and I braced myself for the next battle in the war of our wills.

While I was giving instructions, he left his seat to throw a paper away, crumpling it loudly. Then he went to sharpen his pencil, grinding it down to a nub. Normally I would bristle at such open defiance of class rules. But he was trying to goad me, so I refused to take the bait.

I gave in after he'd disrupted the class for the fourth time in as many minutes. "Jacob, sit down. Don't get out of your chair again. And please see me after class."

He turned and calmly replied, "Fuck you, Mr. Ellison." Then he smiled.

I nodded my head with grim respect. I knew Jacob felt no malice toward me. But he wanted to transfer out of my class, and I wouldn't let him go. This was simply part of his calculated plan to have his way. It was a bold move. It was also unsuccessful. He received a two-day suspension. And the last words he heard as he left the assistant principal's office were, "Mr. Ellison will be eagerly waiting your return."

Jacob was one of my brightest students, and it was clear he enjoyed my classes, especially the debates. But he refused to do homework. In fact, during most of his previous years at school, he had never done any. He had, nonetheless, always managed to slide by with Ds. I wouldn't accept that.

We had many parleys. "Mr. Ellison, I'm not going to do

your homework, no matter what you say. Why won't you just leave me alone?"

"Jacob," I responded, "you're capable of such greatness. I can't sit idly by and allow you to waste so much talent. Besides, my class has rules that all students, including you, must obey. If you don't have your homework tomorrow, then you'll have to stay after school until you complete it."

"I won't stay."

"Then, Jacob, I'll contact your parents."

"Other teachers have called and called. You're wasting your time."

So I visited Jacob's parents at home. No teacher had ever done that before. That's when he asked to switch to another class. He wanted a teacher who would leave him in peace. When the counselor and I refused his request, Jacob plotted his strategy. So far, he was losing the battles. Yet, I certainly wasn't winning the war.

I thought about Jacob a lot during his suspension. Was I trying to force him, a square peg, into my round hole? Could it be that, like Thomas Edison and Albert Einstein, he would never be successful in a conventional school? Perhaps the worst thing I could do was harass him. On the other hand, maybe if I didn't, I'd set him up for disaster in high school. After all, Al Capone probably didn't do too well in school, either. I decided to hold firm. The war resumed right after Jacob returned.

Jacob finally won, of course. He knew I couldn't allow him to constantly disrupt everything for long. He escaped to another teacher who left him alone. Two years later, he dropped out of school.

I still wonder if students, ages hence, will write reports about Jacob's accomplishments. Will he be famous? Or infamous?

I Hate Good-Byes

SOMETIMES I WONDER WHY I TEACH EIGHTH GRADE. I HATE good-byes.

I envy most other teachers who are spared final farewells. For example, although fifth-grade teachers have to watch their students dash out the door for the last time every June, they'll see them again next year, passing in the halls on their way to sixth-grade classes. They can still greet their former students, ask how things are going, offer a little advice, and watch in awe as the kids mature.

When my students celebrate their promotion to high school, however, I have to say good-bye to most of them forever.

On the eve of promotion, I do have one final fling with them: the eighth-grade picnic. It's always a great day full of hot dogs, volleyballs, stolen bases, water balloons, and group photos—all of them silly, joyous reminders of how much I've enjoyed my kids, and how much I'll miss them.

Of course, I shouldn't forget what happened one year—my infamous dive.

I was supposed to supervise the swimming; and I figured, heck, I'm not going to stand around and let the kids have all the fun. So I donned my swimming trunks and headed for the pool. When I arrived, the kids were quite amused to see me so attired. But when I joined the "cool" kids waiting in line to flaunt their stuff off the diving board, they went wild.

"Mr. Ellison's going to dive!" kids screamed throughout the park. They came running from everywhere and lined the fence around the pool. Some cheered. Some laughed. Others stood in stunned disbelief. "Teachers can't swim, can they?"

Well, I've never been able to resist a captive audience. Hamming it up, I went through elaborate stretches, tested the wind direction with my finger, and acted as if I were about to do a triple, inverted somersault with a half-gainer, whatever that is. Of course, all I knew how to do was a regular, head-first dive. I hated to disappoint everybody.

Unfortunately, I didn't. As I ran forward and jumped off my left foot, it slipped out from beneath me. I landed square on my butt, and bounced up high in the air, totally out of control. I came back down onto the board, my arms flailing. For a brief moment, I managed to hang on to the board. But I gradually lost my desperate grip, slipped, and plopped unceremoniously into the water. (The lifeguard made me fill out an accident report afterwards.)

Pandemonium broke loose. Kids rolled on the ground in hysterics. Twice I got back on the board and executed perfect dives. "See! I can do it!"

No one noticed, though, because the kids were still gasping for air between guffaws. In fact, even the next day they burst out laughing when they saw me in the halls. "Gee, Mr. Ellison, can you teach me to dive?" they asked, and then staggered away holding their sides.

I don't know. Maybe it's a good thing I'll never see those kids again.

Get Some Sleep

I USED TO BE IN CONTROL. WHEN I WAS A CLASSROOM TEACHER, I spent endless hours Saturday and Sunday meticulously designing the upcoming week's lessons. I dreaded the painstaking process; and I knew quite well that by Thursday my beautiful plans would probably be shot to hell by the students' unforeseen, sidetracking questions. Nonetheless, once finished, I'd sigh contentedly. I was ready.

Now that I'm an assistant principal, though, my only means of preparing myself for the week—or even for the morrow—is to get enough sleep. You see, I have no idea what challenge may confront me on any given day. I'm almost exclusively reactive, responding to whatever mischief the kids might get themselves into.

One evening last week, for example, I stayed at school late to set up all the student-summons I'd send out first and second periods the following day. I'd finally catch up, clean off my desk!

Then, early the next morning there was a fight at one of the bus stops. I spent an hour and a half getting to the bottom of it, counseling the kids involved, arranging for their punishment, calling their parents. At the end of the day, the neat pile of summons still lay on my now even-messier desk. I'd have to get to them tomorrow—maybe.

To borrow from John Lennon, my life as a new administrator is what happens while I'm busy making other plans. It's frustrating, nerve-wracking, but just as interesting, challenging.

Speaking of fights, I've been amazed at how often kids get themselves into totally irrational, absolutely ridiculous disputes. Several times I've wanted to interrupt their explanations afterwards by shouting, "This is so stupid!" They usually fight with their friends.

I'm beginning to recognize anew how adolescents aren't motivated by thought or reason or any real sense of grievance. They're walking bundles of insecurity and raw emotion, waiting to explode at the slightest provocation. My job is to put them in control of themselves, to show them alternatives to swinging fists, to enable them to make better choices. In this respect, I'm still a teacher.

I've been hindered by some parents, however, who urge their children to resort to violence as the first and only means of resolving problems. "Well, Mr. Ellison, I've always told my son to take down anyone who looks at him funny," one father unabashedly explained. "I won't have a coward for a son."

Unfortunately, "An apple never falls far from the tree." Behind almost every bully is an overbearing mom or dad. Show me an insolent child, and I already know how disrespectfully her parent will respond to my phone call. It's depressing.

I can't take it home, though. There's a certain professional callousness I'll have to develop if I'm to endure. When one young boy ran away from home after I'd suspended him, I was devastated. I blamed myself, certain that a more-experienced administrator would have anticipated it, averted it. I wanted to join the police searching the streets.

"Leave it, Dave," my principal consoled. "This kid's real problems are far more serious than his behavior here at school. They're beyond your powers or responsibilities. Go home and get some rest. Tomorrow other kids will need you."

Indeed. Who knows what the next day might bring?

Real Men Don't Fight

DEAR GREG,

There was no speaking to you after your fight with Andrew yesterday. I tried to reason with you, but you were still too upset.

That's why you have to stay home for the next three days. Yes, your suspension is a punishment. But above all it's an opportunity for you to mull everything over now that you can think more calmly, more clearly. I hope this letter will help.

In some ways, Greg, I don't blame you for going after Andrew. After what he said, why anybody would want to smash him right in the mouth and shut him up. He sure asked for it.

But what did you really accomplish? I suppose you think you defended yourself, protected your honor. You showed Andrew and everyone else that no one can mess with you.

Actually, you did quite the opposite. First of all, you made it clear that you are still such an insecure person, that a few ugly words are enough to make you lose control.

And you know who was in control? Andrew. Think about it. Why would he have sought you out and said what he did, unless he wanted to make you angry? So when you balled your fists and raised your voice, you behaved exactly the way he hoped you would. He played you like a fiddle.

Of course, a crowd of kids—or should I say a mob?—soon gathered to listen to the music. They weren't your friends, though. Friends would have stopped the fight, and saved you from this three-day suspension. No, the kids who came running were no different than a pack of wild dogs, drooling for blood. (Around a fight, everyone begins to act like an animal.) In other words, they were ravenous for some cheap entertainment, and you provided it.

Worst of all, far from putting Andrew in his place, you raised him on high. How? Well, although everybody knows Andrew is a jerk, you made it clear that what he said and thought really mattered to you. You couldn't have paid him a higher compliment.

Greg, even if you still are glad you punched Andrew, just for the emotional satisfaction of having hurt him (not a very nice thing to find out about yourself, is it?), you can't continue to respond that way. After all, you're bound to meet scores of unpleasant people during your life. What are you going to do, punch out every idiot you come across? That would mean you'd always sink to the level of the worst fools around you. And eventually you'd end up in jail.

So the next time somebody tries to goad you into a fight, try a new strategy: Laugh at him. Then turn your back and walk away. That will be the ultimate put-down! Thus, you'll emerge the victor without ever having thrown a punch. And you won't be suspended from school either.

It'll take a lot of self-control, though, a lot of maturity. That's why so few people are capable of doing it. Greg, real men rarely get into a fight. They've learned to solve their problems with their brains, not their fists.

Sweet Kids

When I became assistant principal, I feared I'd learn the names only of the 5 percent or so of the students who misbehave. Would the studious, pleasant, smiling, respectful, silly ones remain strangers to me? It wasn't an encouraging prospect.

So I stuffed my pockets full of Jolly Ranchers, kids' favorite hard candy.

Wherever I wandered during my campus supervision duties, I arbitrarily stopped a child and asked his or her name. I repeated it several times, staring intently at the youngster's bewildered face, and then said, "OK, now I get three strikes. Next time you see me, ask for your name. If I keep forgetting, I'll owe you a Jolly Rancher every time."

Well, the good news is I have managed to learn an awful lot of students' names; and even those children whose names I forget, walk away happy, candy in hand.

Ingenious, right?

Not exactly. The kids whose names I did remember felt cheated. They began to lie about their names, thus confusing me more than ever. Worse, whenever I stepped out of my office, I was beset by a horde of screaming children, their hands outstretched, "What's my name? What's my name? What's my name?"

Several times I had to retreat hastily back to my office for refuge.

I have since changed the rules. Now, in order to earn a candy, students have to first greet me politely, say something complimentary, and only then ask for their name. As a result, the hordes have dwindled and become much more civilized: "Why, good morning, Mr. Ellison. How are you today?" they chant disingenuously. "My, you've got a mighty fine tie on this morning!" I would say that's worth a Jolly Rancher.

Of course, a few miscreants have found a way to foil my plans. "Hey, Mr. Ellison," they smirk, "the top of your head is particularly shiny this morning! Now, what's my name, and where's my candy?"

These may be the same connivers who scammed all of us in the office for a while. You see, we offered candy rewards to any students who turned items in to the lost and found. It was a clever way to battle the finders-keepers-losers-weepers morality of junior high kids.

Well, it didn't take them long to figure out they could simply borrow something from a friend, rush to the office, and with saintly insincerity claim they had found it.

Lest I make anyone believe "kids these days" are an unscrupulous lot, I will end with one more anecdote. Halloween evening I threw a party in my condo's community center. It was fun, but unfortunately I couldn't be home to greet my neighborhood's trick-or-treaters. Instead, I left a large bowl of candy outside my front door. Above it I placed a sign with my apologies, and what I feared would be a futile request to "leave something for the other goblins."

I returned long after midnight to find the bowl still half full.

Who would have thought? Perhaps candy is not really what children crave, but the opportunity to interact with, poke fun at, and every now and then pull a fast one on us adults. Candy is merely their pretext.

That's fine by me because, with every Jolly Rancher, I chuckle with amusement, and may even learn another child's name. So I'll keep my pockets full of candy.

Lies, Lies, Lies

SOMETIMES I FEEL LIKE I MUST HAVE A SIGN ON MY DESK THAT reads, "Assistant Principal: Please lie to me." I have never before endured so many fibs, half-truths, stretched truths, lame excuses, little white lies, and, above all, bald-faced whoppers in my life. Not ten minutes goes by without some student insisting, "I didn't do nothin'!" or "The teacher always picks on me. . . ." or "I guess I forgot, again."

The worst part is how good the kids are at lying—a talent developed after many years of assiduous practice, I assume. They can lie staring me right in the eye, without batting their own, or blushing. They evince no apparent remorse or shame. In fact, they're usually surprised—amused in fact—at my outrage.

Recently, however, I came to understand how some kids have become such good liars. You see, they merely imitate their parents.

This became obvious just prior to Saturday School. Saturday School is punishment for the kids who cut class, or amass more than twelve tardies during a quarter.

The kids' parents had received official notices of the ongoing problem, of course. It was only when the day of reckoning arrived, though, when the letters came informing the parents they'd have to get their children to school on Saturday and so be inconvenienced themselves that many parents finally took notice.

Then came their barrage of phone calls laden with clever explanations for the children's misbehavior. Thus the parents modeled how lying for expediency's sake, to avoid the consequences of your own actions, for example, is perfectly acceptable. Their kids watched and learned, only too well.

Perhaps that's why I was so impressed by and concerned for Dominic, a cute fifth grader who showed up in my office one afternoon, his head hung in shame. He'd been involved in a shoving match with another, bigger kid, and had ended up punching him furiously, futilely. With uncommon, naive candor he fessed up to his crime. The other boy cunningly denied everything, claiming he'd just been standing there, minding his own business. . . .

Dominic's eyes grew wide with wonder, then anger, then tears. What a terrible lesson he was learning! As there were no witnesses to the incident, my course of action as assistant principal was clear: I'd have to punish Dominic, and let the other boy go, scott free. It was intolerable, but inevitable.

Well, you can believe I was more than merciful with Dominic; and concluded with a long sermon—glancing periodically at the other boy—about how proud I was of Dominic for his honesty; how he'd be able to look at himself in the mirror and know he'd guarded his honor, preserved his integrity, and earned my respect. He was a real man.

All I had to offer were words, sincere but empty words, in a callous world, which rewards only guile, where good guys usually finish last.

It's never been harder to be virtuous, I suppose; nor more challenging to raise virtuous children. Dominic and his loving mother prove it is possible. But, oh how special, how fragile they are! We must celebrate them, nurture them, wonder at them, and pray that within their singular hearts yet thrives a nobility that can somehow, someday, redeem us all.

A Box of Oreos

FRANCIS WAS PATHETIC. ONE DREARY, DANK MORNING HE SLIPPED on the bus, bouncing down the steps to land with an awkward plop on the sidewalk. He sat and cried—not from pain or embarrassment, but from utter despair. He was the most unhappy boy I'd ever met.

A crack, fetal-alcohol infant, Francis had been snatched out of the arms of his prostitute mother. Two years later, the police had broken down the door of his foster home to find him alone in a filthy sty, eating his own feces.

Now he lived with Mrs. Flemming (not her real name), an unscrupulous viper who claimed the dubious title of Francis' "mother." She didn't cook for him regularly, or wash his clothes, or ensure he'd bathed or done his homework. Often, in fact, she locked him out on the streets until late at night. About the only thing she did well was collect the Social Services check every month, and coach Francis on how to respond to any pesky assistant principal's probing questions.

I liked Francis, pitied him, too often lost my temper with him, but still greeted him at the buses with an arm around his tiny shoulders, and a chipper, "Good morning, Francis! Now, what kind of day are you going to have?"

Often his shoulders shook with rage, and I'd banish him to my office until he calmed down enough to report to class. Nonetheless, by recess he'd usually said something awful, got lots of other kids good and mad, and then retaliated to their gibes with his tiny fists.

He was a menace, especially to himself, as his "victims" were often three times his size. It was only a matter of time before Francis really hurt someone, or, more likely, somebody really hurt him.

Desperate, I called Social Services. "Francis? Francis who?" the clerk responded. She had no record of him. I nagged, phoning every day until finally a social worker met with me and a reluctant Mrs. Flemming. Afterwards, he turned to me and, shaking his head, whispered grimly, "I don't have any place else to send him, but document everything anyway."

I did. The last straw, however, didn't occur until January.

Francis had been absent several days in a row, which was unlike him. On the fourth morning, he'd tumbled out of the school bus looking even more disheveled than usual. I'd expected his typical pat, rehearsed answers in my office, but this time Francis broke down: He let it slip that he'd spent the last three nights in a shed, with nothing more than a blanket and a box of Oreos.

Mrs. Flemming hadn't reported him missing to anyone. Had she even noticed? I reached for the phone.

That evening the police dragged Francis away kicking and screaming from the only home he'd ever known. "My God," I shuddered, "what have I done?" And that was the last I saw or heard of him. That is, until last week. Francis phoned from out of the blue, and left a message with his number.

"Sorry, Francis is at wrestling practice," the group home counselor responded when I called, breathless.

"He wrestles?" I stuttered incredulously.

"Well, yes, but actually his favorite sport is soccer."

So, perhaps God has smiled on Francis at last.

Frankenstein

"I WISH HE WOULD JUST KILL HIMSELF," MATT'S DAD EXCLAIMED when I informed him of his son's expulsion. Another father responded similarly, lashing out at his tearful daughter, Anna, "Why won't you just run away?" Jimmy, whom I suspect I'll expel before June, has only one thing to say to me, ever: "I don't care."

I believe him. Why should he care about anyone or anything, least of all himself, given that nobody significant in his life has ever cared for him? He's been tossed like a hot potato from one reluctant family member to another. He knows he's bad. He's accepted with an eerie stoicism that life, too, is awful, and likely to remain so.

These profoundly unhappy kids—and so many others in schools throughout this nation—are bright, beautiful, and, I suspect, clinically depressed. I've referred them to a therapist who counsels them periodically here on campus, both individually and in groups. They discuss anger control, even though they have many legitimate, horrific reasons to be furious. They speak of self-esteem, even though their experience has thoroughly convinced them they are worthless.

"What do you want?" desperately, repeatedly I ask them. And then, to fill their ominous silence, I plead, "Whatever it is, don't lose sight of it! Make your decisions carefully so you won't throw it away. You can be master of your fate . . ."

Nonetheless, with few exceptions, such kids spurn my advice, sabotage any possibility for happiness. They simply loathe themselves and their lives too much. Indeed, they're quite clever about putting me in a position where I must punish them, even kick them out of school, and thus become an unwitting accomplice in their unconscious, self-destructive designs.

Ultimately many will commit suicide—slowly, with alcohol, with drugs, with unprotected sex, with gangs, with crime. Or, like Eric Harris and Dylan Klebold at Columbine High School, a few will end their lives in a violent rampage.

You see, those boys were hardly unique. They were but a sensational, gruesome tip of an untold iceberg of "outcast" children in our society, some of whom grace my office daily, most of whom either already populate our burgeoning prisons or soon will. They don't all wear black trench coats. However, so many have grown up essentially orphans, lacking one decent adult who might have spent time with them, listened to their dreams, set some sane limits, who should have told them daily in both word and deed, "I love you."

Without such nurturing—which neither a therapist nor I can magically provide now—children grow up spiritually withered, twisted, deformed.

I cannot condemn the two Colorado boys—or the kids I expel from school such as Matt, Anna, and Jimmy. The boys were monsters, yes, but they also were victims. My God, who filled their young hearts with such hatred for others and themselves? Who taught them to fire an assault rifle or make a propane bomb? Who left them alone, with enough unsupervised time to meticulously plan such an unspeakable act of nihilism and despair?

Such kids and such catastrophes do not arise spontaneously. Like Frankenstein, we create them. And it will take a lot more than shaking our heads in feigned disbelief to wash our hands of their blood, or the blood they spill.

Tears

MARCELA WOULD CRY BEFORE THE END OF FIRST PERIOD.

At 7:45 A.M., she hastened as best she could across the school courtyard, heavily laden with books, papers, and boxes for the morning's lesson. She spied what she thought was help: four of her best students in conversation with the principal.

"Are these your kids?" the principal queried with a frown.

"Why, yes, of course. What's wrong?"

"We can't tell you," whispered one of Marcela's students, "but it's not good."

The same four students looked up in alarm only ten minutes later when the phone interrupted the lesson. They gave each other furtive, knowing glances, then looked guiltily down. Marcela answered the phone with a sense of dread. It was the principal. The police wanted to speak to the students. Send them to the office, now.

Shaking with apprehension, Marcela did her best to carry on, but wondered how long she could. This couldn't have come on a worse day. You see, it was the Friday before Mother's Day—a holiday that had ceased to be a joyous event seven years before, when Marcela's only daughter, Erika, had died in an automobile accident. Mother's Day served only to heighten her grief, to remind her cruelly that she once had been a mother, but was no more, save for her students. Now four of them—her babies!—were in serious trouble, and once again she was powerless to protect them.

"Oh God, please no! No! Help them, please," she prayed silently.

However, her prayers were futile, apparently, because there stood the principal at the door, her eyes glaring, her arms sternly crossed.

Then, in paraded the four students, one carrying balloons, another flowers, another a breakfast of fruit and bagels, and the last a giant card signed by all of Marcela's children. "Happy Mother's Day!" they screamed with glee.

That's when Marcela broke down and sobbed.

In the center of the card appeared a poem by Theresa Langdon, which the kids had altered a bit for Marcela: "It's Mothers Day and we wanted to be sure you know how very glad we are that you are our teacher . . . Our lives have been enriched because you have been there to comfort us, to encourage us, to hug us . . ."

Around the poem, every child had written a personal note such as this one:

You are a great teacher! You are like my second mother. . . .

Then, in a small, scrawled afterthought,

P.S. I'll try not to talk too much, but don't think I can. . . .

Marcela laughed through her tears.

When she'd calmed down many hours afterward, she accosted me.

"You're going to write about this, Dave! Every day we have to read horrific news about a few bad kids, such as the two in Colorado who killed others, then themselves. But what about the rest of them, most of them, who are wonderful?

"This," she said tremulously, pointing to the posterboard card, "is only one of many wonderful things kids do, a sample of how sensitive they can be, and how caring. Perhaps if we told such stories more often, people would believe in children, and children could believe in themselves."

Indeed.

"I felt really good about doing it," explained one of Marcela's children. "It made me feel great to see my teacher so happy."

Maybe we should all cry.

Take a Big Breath

DEAR HIGH SCHOOL STUDENTS,

Why does someone have to die for you to learn how to live?

Last week, I attended Erika's funeral. Along with her friend, Ed, she died after a terrible traffic accident. Like most of you, I didn't know Erika or Ed. But Erika's mom is my colleague and my friend, so the tragedy was more than just a headline for me.

I wish it could be for all of you, too; because if Erika and Ed's apparently senseless deaths are to have any meaning at all, it will be because you teenagers learn from them. So, for the sake of Erika, Ed, their parents and friends, take heed:

In your eagerness to enjoy all the rights and pleasures of an adult, don't forget the awesome responsibility that accompanies them. For example, with your physical maturity comes the ability to create life; and with your car keys the power to destroy it.

It might have been any of you behind the wheel of the truck that drove Erika and Ed to their deaths. So far, you've been lucky. If you are to remain so, you must recognize that an automobile isn't an exciting toy, to be loaned around for all to try. It's a weapon more deadly than any handgun. The next time you grip a steering wheel, remember you have the lives of all of us in your hands.

Also, recall that you yourself are not immortal. Psychologists say it's normal (but dangerous) for you to believe you are exempt from the consequences of your silly, thoughtless deeds. "It can't happen to me," you say. That's exactly what Erika and Ed thought as they climbed into the back of the truck and, just that once, didn't wear seatbelts. Perhaps now you'll realize that life is for real, and shows no mercy. Often you don't get a second chance.

Erika's parents placed many tender letters of love in their daughter's coffin. The letters were beautiful, and yet sad gestures. They expressed all the praise and affection Erika's friends had never gotten around to saying while Erika was still alive. What a shame!

Fate is fickle, you know, and might have chosen one of your friends instead. Take a moment today to think of those you love, but take for granted. Imagine all the wonderful things you'd want to say to them in a letter if they were to be suddenly taken away. Then write and send that letter now. I think Erika and Ed would like that.

There's one last thing I urge you to ponder: When Erika's friends gave some short, emotional eulogies at the funeral, they said things like, "She had such a sunny smile!" and "I could always count on her!" No one mentioned stylish clothes, a slim figure, or a flashy car, even though our TV-influenced culture claims they are so important. At a grave we recall what really matters.

The trouble is that you teenagers forget the lessons of death. It seems a youngster has to die each year for you to pause, and remember. (Some of you, like the two who rode to Erika's funeral in the back of a pickup, don't get it even then!) That's why I wanted to write you about Erika and Ed. I don't want to bury any more of you.

So, take a deep breath. Celebrate life. Cherish each other. And please be careful.

Glass Half Full

I WAS DUMBSTRUCK. THEY WEREN'T AT ALL WHAT I HAD EXPECTED.

The first, a tall girl in a pretty dress, portrayed a dialogue between two women, both accused of witchcraft. One instant, she'd wring her hands, her voice young and terrified, pleading for mercy. The next, she'd fold her hands in calm, resigned despair, and intone piously, "I will not lie to save my life—or yours." Finally, in a fit of hysterical, cowardly lies, the first woman condemned her friend to the flames, but saved herself.

Then the actress was silent. She smiled briefly, and sat down. My jaw hung open.

A young man took her place, and transported me from seventeenth-century Salem to twentieth-century Auschwitz. His hands too, collaborated in a terrifying conversation. At first his fingers fluttered effeminately about, seeming to caress each tender, yet courageous word: "Why do you wear the Jewish star instead of a pink triangle like me?" Then the hands dropped rigidly at the youngster's side, while his now harsh, remorseless voice replied that he had raped a dead Jewish girl, just to prove to his Nazi captors that he really wasn't homosexual. He would do anything to survive, even betray his trusting lover.

When that actor finally sat down, I was emotionally exhausted. But three contestants still waited their turn!

The most torturous moment, however, occurred when all five kids had finished, and I had to judge them. One must be best, one second-best . . . and one worst. Impossible! Virtually all the dramatic interpretations had been simply superb. How could I decide?

Meanwhile, more than a hundred other volunteer judges agonized just as I did. Together, choosing from among the 275 high school contestants at the regional forensics competition, we'd determine the lucky few who would go on to the state finals.

In the next round, I judged oratorical interpretation, and it went no better. One orator became Gandhi, standing stolidly before a British court, denouncing imperialism. Another re-created Jesse Jackson's famous "Common Ground" speech that appealed for solidarity among all peoples. The third, a fire-and-brimstone preacher, his eyes blazing and finger pointing, assured me that I was about to crash the ship of my soul onto the rocks of Perdition.

Once again I was enthralled by the speeches, but bewildered by my still-empty scorecard. It was a long, grueling day.

Nonetheless, now that it's over, I am filled with a tremendous sense of pride and optimism. It's so easy to believe "kids these days" are hoodlums. Today, though, I witnessed a seemingly endless parade of inspiring young men and women. They brought to life and reveled in some of the most beautiful, most powerful words in the English language. In doing so, they demonstrated remarkable intelligence, uncommon motivation, and admirable character. No matter how I had to judge them, they were all winners.

These students may not make headlines. But it is they, not the hoodlums, who will one day lead this nation. They provide proof that the glass of American youth is, indeed, at least half full.

An Angel Named Ramu

CHRISTMAS ANGELS SPOKE TO ME RECENTLY, THROUGH THE MOUTH of a young Indian boy named Ramu.

I'd needed the angels' grace. You see, it's been a difficult first year as assistant principal for me. One afternoon when I was on lunch supervision duty, for example, I realized I'd spent the entire hour chastising kids. My face was set in a severe frown. My blood pressure was noticeably high. And I thought to myself with a mixture of alarm and despair, "What's happening to me? I used to like kids, joke with them, attempt to inspire them. . . ."

Which is why I treasured the meeting in my office with Ramu. A fifth grader, he'd been having an ongoing problem with some fellow immigrant, Mexican American children. They had been insulting him and his Indian friends with the epithet "Gandhi." (Many immigrants, ever-insecure, look for some victim even lower on the social scale than they, so quite often ridicule and harass each other.)

I'd sent summons for Ramu, two of his friends, and four of their tormentors. Six waited, fidgeting nervously in my cramped office, eyeing each other warily. The seventh hadn't yet arrived. During the interlude, I engaged Ramu in small talk, learning that he had "tree" brothers and sisters.

"Three," I responded. "Thhhhhhhhhhhhhreeeeee. You have to place your tongue beneath your teeth and then blow some air. Thhhhhhhhhhhreeeee." By the time the seventh student finally arrived, I had all the kids—Indian and Mexican alike—

sticking their tongues out, blowing air, practicing, laughing: "Thhhhhhis. Thhhhhat. Thhhhhese. Thhhhhose. Thhhhhreee. Thhhhirteen. . . ."

Thus, inadvertently, I'd made my first point, that these boys had a lot in common, not the least of which was their struggle to learn English.

Finally we got to the matter at hand. Yes, the Mexican kids admitted they'd called the Indians "Gandhi." Did they know who Gandhi was? No. I asked Ramu to explain, and he did so with charming enthusiasm.

"Now isn't it silly," I asked the Mexican boys, "for you to use such an impressive man's name as an insult?" They nodded sheepishly. "And didn't you know that even César Chávez admired Gandhi, used him as his model?" No, they didn't know that either.

When the Indian boys revealed they'd never heard of Chávez, the Mexicans launched into their own passionate lesson. The interview ended with all seven boys shaking each other's hands, timidly, but with cautious grins. Their punishment: to have lunch together and discuss their respective heroes further.

For that one, brief moment, I felt really good about my job as assistant principal.

The following evening I was once again on supervision duty, this time at the choir's winter concert. There in the first row stood little Ramu, joyfully singing traditional Christmas songs, a Mexican lullaby, and a Jewish prayer. "Only in America," I mused with pride, "can an Indian boy learn to sing unabashedly in English, Spanish, and Hebrew!"

As Ramu belted out the concert's finale, "Angels We Have Heard on High," I recalled the meeting I'd had with him the day before in my office—the United Nations of students at my school—and all the challenges and opportunities they create; and I realized that, through children like Ramu, the angels of Bethlehem still proclaim their eternal promise of hope: "Peace on Earth! Goodwill towards men!"

Beardless, But Still Trying to Help

I'VE LOST MY BEARD. A FEW MONTHS AGO THE STUDENTS AT MY school undertook a pizza fund-raiser. As an incentive, I agreed to shave if they met what I hoped would prove an impossible goal. Well, the little buggers made it.

When the accursed day of reckoning finally arrived, a committee of overeager miscreants tracked me down during lunch, and dragged me out to the courtyard. There a merciless barber stood grinning cruelly.

I hammed it up and pretended to struggle tooth and nail. At one moment I even slipped from the committee's grasp and dashed away, pursued by hundreds of shrieking kids. I let them catch me, of course, and then bravely faced my executioner.

You would think the students would appreciate this supreme sacrifice of mine. But no, ever-devious, at the last moment they instructed the barber to shave only the left half of my beard. I had to walk around the rest of the day looking completely ridiculous.

Speaking of missing hair . . . a new student—a cute immigrant girl from China—knocked meekly at my office door recently. She inquired about a small, red placard hanging on the wall across from my desk. I'd obtained it during an Asian Pride Week, when Chinese students were creating such placards for everyone. They'd write whatever you wanted in beautiful Chinese calligraphy. I'd asked them to put "Welcome," and I've hung the placard proudly in my classroom—and now my office—for years.

I pointed toward it and grinned broadly at the timid girl. "Do you like it? Welcome! Welcome!"

She shook her head ominously, and a dull knot of anxiety formed in my stomach. "It does say that," I gulped, "doesn't it?"

"No, it say, 'Man with bald head.'"

"Why those rotten . . . ," I muttered, gnashing my teeth. Nonetheless, I've left the placard right where it was. I've decided I like it now more than ever.

Many of my best efforts seem to end in disasters like that. I recall, for example, one instance when I tried to assist a woman in the office. I'd come up behind her at the front counter, and I could tell she was furious.

I quickly learned she'd had a bitter argument with her daughter the night before. The third day of our Spirit Week, everyone was supposed to wear their pajamas to school, and thus, in a silly, fun way, show their school spirit. Evidently, the daughter had decided her normal PJs just weren't good enough. She'd insisted on some new, expensive, flashy ones. The mother had ultimately acquiesced, but now seemed to have regretted it. She blamed the school for the whole mess. "This stupid Pajama Day ruined my relationship with my daughter!" she complained for the whole office to hear. "Which is not even to mention the money I wasted!"

I stepped next to her and proffered, "Good morning, Ma'am. I'm Mr. Ellison, an assistant principal here. Can I be of assistance?"

She turned and eyed me standing there in my full-length plaid flannel nightgown. Rolling her eyes, she threw her arms up in exasperation, screamed "Aaaagggh!" and stormed out.

I was just trying to help . . .

My Lesson

When does compassion become enabling? How do you reconcile one student's needs with those of the entire school?

I'm facing these issues more and more lately as students I like and care for very much reach the end of their rope— usually a long one, which I've naively handed them, and which, unfortunately, they've used to hang themselves.

Sylvia, for example, transferred to my school from another district several years ago. She caused nothing but trouble. At the beginning of this academic year my principal had finally had enough. She decided to deny Sylvia's transfer.

When I learned of the girl's pathetic home life, however, I argued on her behalf. (I'm a new assistant principal, you see.) "She's going to counseling," I pleaded. "She's trying. Let me give her another chance. I'll put her on a special, strict contract."

The principal, who's seen many such students come and go over the years, rolled her eyes, but acquiesced. "OK, Dave. But she'll be your responsibility, your problem—and ultimately, your lesson."

Ha! I eagerly met in September with Sylvia and her current guardian, Grandma, and informed them I'd won Sylvia a reprieve. But, she'd either have to behave or I'd revoke her interdistrict transfer.

Well, a few weeks ago Sylvia earned her twenty-seventh referral to my office. She'd once more mouthed off to a teacher. The trouble was, I knew why. Sylvia had visited her parents the day before. They'd just been evicted. In their final hour at the house, with Sylvia watching, they systematically destroyed the place in a violent, drunken rampage. They ruined everything, even the things Sylvia had left behind when she'd gone to live with her grandmother.

No wonder Sylvia was so angry! No wonder she'd lashed out at the first person who crossed her the next day! I couldn't bring myself to send her away. Instead, I suspended her again, and gave her yet another chance.

The principal responded afterwards with a terse, exasperated memo: "Truly, David, there will always be some excuse for Sylvia's behavior. At what point does she take responsibility for her actions? In some ways, we are teaching her that she never has to behave because her home life is so terrible."

Hmmmm. I wanted so badly for Sylvia to succeed, despite the rotten hand life had dealt her. Nonetheless, there were only too many other similar children for whom the best thing my school offered was a safe haven away from their parents. And most of those kids amazingly managed to keep themselves under control. What message did I send them by coddling Sylvia? What message did I send her?

A week later Sylvia lost it again in class. I liked her. I pitied her. And I expelled her.

A colleague of mine remarked recently how my year as assistant principal has changed me: "You're a lot more strict, Dave. You don't laugh as much as you used to. I suppose that comes with the job."

Indeed. Every day I'm learning to embrace the concept of "tough love," to compassionately mete out severe consequences for kids' poor choices. Sometimes a crisis is exactly what they (and their parents) need.

It's a lesson I'd rather not have learned, though, and one I'd rather not have to teach.

The King of Children

DECREPIT, POL POT EMERGED FROM THE JUNGLE. RELUCTANT, Swiss banks acknowledged their Nazi complicity. Shamefaced, German Chancellor Herzotg visited the U.S. National Holocaust Museum. 1995 provided a summer to contemplate the horror of genocide, the dark night of the human soul manifest so starkly this century.

And yet, while humans are capable of such unspeakable degradation, we can also exhibit unimaginable self-sacrifice. In fact, it is usually at a moment of unmitigated madness that, like a diamond in the rough, the magnificence of the human spirit shines forth. Such was the life and martyrdom of Janusz Korczak. You see, he was The King of Children.

Korczak's real name was Henryk Goldszmit; but most of Europe still knows him by his pen name, Korczak. At the age of five he chose his life's path, vowing naively to end the suffering of the innumerable miserably poor children he saw in Warsaw.

Years later, while still a young medical student, he wandered through the city's worst neighborhoods, treating and encouraging the pitiful children he found. He came to love them.

"When the devil will we stop prescribing aspirin for poverty, exploitation, lawlessness, and crime?" he complained. In 1910 Korczak abandoned his lucrative medical career and built the first of his orphanages. He made it a "Children's Republic," empowering his youthful charges radically: They chose their own goals, operated their own court, and even published their own newspaper, which eventually found a national audience.

"Children . . . are people," he argued. "Not people-to-be, not people of tomorrow, but people now, right now—today." He held them to strict academic and ethical standards, pioneering a moral pedagogy that became a model for the nation's schools. Teachers ought to be, he maintained, "the sculptor of the child's soul."

One orphan still recalls his first day at the orphanage. He'd earned a reputation for being a ruffian, incorrigible. Nonetheless, Korczak gave him the nickname "Stasiek." "I really liked that name—a saint's name. 'What, me have a name like that?' I said. 'Yes, you.' By that act he became my best friend."

In the 1930's, Korczak had a national radio program. Calling himself The Old Doctor, "he dispensed homey wisdom and wry humor. Somehow, listening to his deceptively simple words made his listeners feel like better people."* Eventually he published more than twenty-four books and one thousand news and magazine articles, winning Poland's most prestigious literary awards, and earning a fame similar to that of America's Dr. Spock and Dr. Seuss.

In 1939, however, Germany invaded Poland. Korczak, alias Goldszmit, was a Jew. Most of his orphans were Jewish. When the Nazis forced them into the Ghetto, he went with them. And when the kids were eventually herded off to the cattle cars, he spurned many opportunities to save himself, and marched serenely at their head. "You do not leave a sick child in the night," he explained, "and you do not leave children at a time like this."

Janusz Korczak, along with two hundred of his beloved children, was gassed at Treblinka.

In an era when life was cheap, Korczak reminded us which lives were most precious. Now, when we recall the Holocaust, let us also remember Korczak—his selflessness, his wisdom, and his cause.

---

*The King of Children, A Biography of Janusz Korczak *by Betty Jean Lifton, was published in 1988 by Schocken Books, Inc., New York.*

An Answer, Finally

DEAR IMELDA,

I owe you an answer, even after all these years, and even though you probably have forgotten you ever asked me the question. Perhaps you don't even remember me, your sixth-grade teacher. But I haven't forgotten you or your question, or the year we spent together in that sweltering Texas classroom. How could I forget my first year of teaching?

My friends had told me that my first year would be hell, and they weren't mistaken. I slaved each evening over homework and quiz papers. I sacrificed my weekends to create beautifully intricate lesson plans, only to abandon them by Wednesday. Worse, I did not yet know how to manage a classroom or discipline teenagers. Indeed, my voice was usually hoarse at the end of each day—not from lecturing, but from yelling and screaming, all to no avail.

The worst time, as you may recall, Imelda, was just after lunch. The class would return from recess all sweaty and excited, in no mood to be quiet or cooperate with anyone. Row by row, I would dismiss you to the rest rooms. I needed to supervise the classroom, the water fountains, and the rest rooms, all simultaneously. I usually wasn't very successful. (If only I had a dime for every water fight that took place that year!) And all the while I kept thinking to myself, "This isn't what I had in mind when I chose to become a teacher." Oh how I hated that quarter hour just after lunch!

It was at just such a moment that you asked me your question, Imelda. You must have noticed my impatient, anguished frustration. (Even now I still can't hide my moods from my students.) I wonder how long you watched me before you asked, "Mr. Ellison, are you happy?"

It was such a simple, yet profound question—the kind only the youth in all your innocence can ask. It caught me by surprise. "Right now, I really don't know," I responded lamely. Then I tried to turn the tables: "How about you, Imelda? Are you happy?"

Without a moment's hesitation you matter-of-factly responded, "Yes, Mr. Ellison, I am." And that was the end of our conversation.

Twenty years have swept by, Imelda. By now you're a woman—an engineer? A mother? A teacher? I, too, have grown up. I've lost a lot of hair, but learned a great deal about teaching. For example, I never lose my temper anymore. (Well, almost never.)

Over the years, I've taught several thousand students. Many of them I've already forgotten. But, as I said, Imelda, I haven't forgotten you, or your question. I've always felt uncomfortable about my inability to respond as quickly or sincerely as you. Now, at last, it is fitting that I finally do. I was going to qualify my answer with "All things considered . . ." or "Overall . . ." But your simple question deserves better than that.

Yes, Imelda, I am happy. And wherever you are, I hope you still are too.

"Isn't that right, Mr. Ellison?"

FATHER KIRBY'S PHOTOGRAPH APPEARED ON THE FINAL PAGE OF my high school's newsletter. He still wore the same white lab coat, and seemed on the verge of yet another dissertation on the intricacies of subatomic particles. I quickly scanned the accompanying column for news of his latest accomplishment, only to learn he had recently passed away.

I hadn't thought of Father Kirby once during the many years since I'd left his high school physics class. Nonetheless, I sat for a long time and sadly reminisced.

I wondered if he'd remembered me. I was the short kid who sat in the first row, just by the door. I had a habit of falling asleep almost every day. (That's why Father Kirby sat me in front.) I couldn't help it! No matter which class I had after lunch, I would always nod off for fifteen minutes or so. Every once in a while Father Kirby would awaken me with a loud, "Isn't that right, Mr. Ellison?"

I'd blurt out a confused, "Yes, sir!" Usually, I'd just agreed to something quite absurd, and everyone would laugh. I deserved it.

He probably thought I hated physics. Actually, it was my favorite class. I had always been bored with math. The equations seemed to have no purpose or practical application. I merely plugged in the numbers mechanically, disinterestedly.

Father Kirby, though, taught me to use those apparently meaningless equations to precisely describe the world around me, and even to accurately predict how worlds light years away must behave. I marveled that all the galaxies paid homage to the same mathematical laws. In short, I was fascinated. (At least when I wasn't snoring.) I wish I'd told him so.

I recalled one day when Kirby had supervision duty during lunch. He paced up and down the aisles of tables, oblivious to the din, lost in thought. I watched him make one circuit around the cafeteria, and wondered: What was it like to be a priest, without a family? Was he lonely? Didn't he get tired of conducting the same experiments year after year? What did he do for fun? (Did he ever have fun?)

For that one, brief instant, I possessed enough maturity to see Father Kirby as a person. I realized I liked him. The moment of insight passed, though, and I went back to throwing my Jell-O across the table.

On the last day of school, Father Kirby offered us seniors some sage advice (which we promptly forgot), and wished us all a heartfelt good-bye. Then the final bell rang. Why didn't we stop to thank him, or at least shake his hand? Instead, with a joyous "Free at last!" we dashed out without so much as a glance in his direction. We left him in that silent classroom, to muse on our ingratitude, alone.

Now, so many years later, I finally recognize my debt to Father Kirby. But, of course, it's too late for a belated "Thank you." What a shame.

I suppose it's only normal. After all, my students are no different. I can only hope that a few of them will remember me likewise one day. Perhaps there'll even be one who will become a teacher, and honor me, just as I will try to honor Father Kirby: She will carry on.

"Isn't that right, Ms. Fletcher?"